M &

M & E Handbooks are recommended reading for examination syllabuses all over the world. Because each Handbook covers its subject clearly and concisely books in the series form a vital part of many college, university, school and home study courses.

Handbooks contain detailed information stripped of unnecessary padding, making each title a comprehensive self-tuition course. They are amplified with numerous self-testing questions in the form of Progress Tests at the end of each chapter, each text-referenced for easy checking. Every Handbook closes with an appendix which advises on examination techniques. For all these reasons, Handbooks are ideal for pre-examination revision.

The handy pocket-book size and competitive price make Handbooks the perfect choice for anyone who wants to grasp the essentials of a subject quickly and easily.

Other M & E books of interest:

HANDBOOKS
Basic Accounting
Intermediate Accounts
Principles of Accounts

BECBOOKS
Accounting Level II
Accounting Level III

FREDbooks
Fred Learns Book-keeping

THE M & E HANDBOOK SERIES

Basic
Book-keeping

J O Magee, FCA

Formerly Principal Lecturer in Accountancy at the
Polytechnic of North London

SECOND EDITION

Pitman Publishing
128 Long Acre, London WC2E 9AN

First published 1972
Reprinted 1973, 1975, 1976
Second edition 1979
Reprinted 1980, 1983, 1986, 1987

© Macdonald & Evans Ltd 1979

ISBN 0-7121-0274-4

Founding Editor: P W D Redmond

Printed and bound in Great Britain by
Richard Clay Ltd, Bungay, Suffolk

PREFACE

The object of this **HANDBOOK** is to show how logic and simplicity can be applied simultaneously to the recording of business transactions by means of double-entry book-keeping. Its common-sense approach provides the student with a clear explanation of events enabling him to appreciate *why* things should be done and, at the same time, *how* they are to be done. Because the approach is simple, interest is readily stimulated and the student should quickly obtain a sound grasp of the basic elements of the subject. Since accountancy is based entirely on double-entry book-keeping it follows that a mastery of the subject is absolutely essential if the student intends to progress to higher studies. This basis is a vital prerequisite for *all examinations in book-keeping and accounting* and this book sets out to provide that base.

During the past twenty years or so the introductory teaching of book-keeping has swung away from the somewhat pedestrian and unimaginative approach which had been employed since time immemorial. The modern way of teaching the subject is to introduce the balance sheet in some form or other at the very start of study and this does indeed appear to be a considerable improvement on the old method. In this book I have presented the subject with this in mind although, like other writers, I have my own ideas about how a real understanding of principles can best be implanted in the mind of the student. The method shown in this book was developed over a period of some ten years; it did not just evolve overnight. Since the middle 'fifties I have used it with very satisfactory results and I feel, therefore, that I can safely offer it to students wishing to study the subject.

In conjunction with *Basic Accounting* (to be published in the **HANDBOOK** series) this book provides full cover for the syllabuses of the main examining bodies at elementary and intermediate levels as well as giving a very sound base for the examinations of the leading professional bodies.

July 1972   J. O. MAGEE

PREFACE TO THE SECOND EDITION

The second edition of this **HANDBOOK** contains all the
material of the original edition to which I have added a chapter
entitled "Moving Towards Accountancy." The idea is to introduce the student to one particular aspect of the possibilities
which may be open to those whose interest has been stimulated
by the logic of double-entry book-keeping.

These days we frequently read in the newspapers and hear on
the radio and television the expression "cash flow". This is a
term which was introduced from the U.S.A. some years ago and
which, by now, has become fashionable not merely in accounting circles but among the general public. The expression "he is
having cash flow problems" has become something of a cliché,
the inference being that, far from there being any flow of cash,
the contrary is the case. Debtors are failing to pay their bills
and as a result there is a chain reaction of liabilities.

In this new chapter I have tried to show how to diagnose at
which points a business is experiencing difficulty and where
remedial action can be applied. It may be that a firm's current
assets are not being used with due economy and that benefits
can be obtained by a proper analysis of the causes of such mis-
use. From a reading of this chapter it is hoped that students
will be directed into the path of useful enquiry and at the same
time will gain some insight into the possibilities which lie ahead
of them in the accounting field.

October 1978   J. O. MAGEE

CONTENTS

CHAPTER I

THE THEORY UPON WHICH
BOOK-KEEPING IS BASED

BUSINESS TRANSACTIONS

1. Introduction. Before any rational discussion of book-keeping can be entered into it is essential that the meaning of certain basic matters be explained. If this is not done at the very beginning newcomers to the subject may find themselves in difficulties. Tutors sometimes—in all innocence let it be said —take it for granted that certain terms, simple enough to the initiated, are understood by the beginner as a matter of course. Quite often, unfortunately, this is not the case and as a result no explanation is offered. The consequence, all too often, is that the student, not wishing to appear stupid in front of his class, remains silent. Thus, from the very beginning of his study of the subject he finds himself living in a world of uncertainty, always hoping that before the next lesson he may have managed to find somebody who can help him solve his difficulty. This only happens to the lucky ones.

No apology is made, therefore, for putting first things first and for attempting to explain those matters which seem to be of real importance before any serious study of the subject can begin. Consequently, in the first two chapters we will explain, among other matters, the meaning of certain terms which are commonly used in book-keeping so that this will smooth the way for what follows.

2. Double-entry book-keeping. This is the title given to a particular technique by means of which business transactions are recorded. From these records the profit (or loss) made by a business during a period of trading may be ascertained; in addition, a summary setting out its general situation can be readily produced. With the recording of each transaction the *history* of the business is gradually built up.

From the study of past records the owner of a business

should be able to plan his future activities in the expectation that beneficial results may follow. In this way the *past* may be used as a springboard for the *future*.

3. The requirements of a business transaction. Three essentials are needed to complete a business transaction. These are:

(*a*) at least two parties must be involved;
(*b*) there must be

    (*i*) the transfer of goods from one person to the other, or
    (*ii*) the performance of a service by one of the parties for the benefit of the other;

(*c*) there must be payment (or some other mutually satisfactory form of settlement) for the goods or for the service performed.

4. The twin aspects of a business transaction. As was stated in 3(*a*) at least two persons are required for a transaction to be carried out. Consider the following circumstances:

Robert is in need of a pair of shoes and goes into a shop belonging to George. He tells George what he requires. Sitting down he takes off one of his shoes and his measurements are taken. This done, several boxes of shoes are brought for Robert to try on. At length he finds a pair which suit him and George tells him that they cost £5. Robert agrees to buy them for that sum. The shoes are then wrapped up and handed to Robert who, in turn, gives £5 to George. This completes the transaction.

From this simple illustration we can see that the twin elements of *giving* and *receiving* are both present in the transaction:

(*a*) George *gives* Robert a pair of shoes,
(*b*) Robert *receives* a pair of shoes.

Thus George *loses* and Robert *gains*. But this, of course, is not the end of the matter since:

(*c*) Robert then *gives* George £5,
(*d*) George *receives* £5.

Now it is the turn of Robert *to lose* and George *to gain* and in this way equilibrium is restored.

5. Giving and receiving. It must be clearly understood that for something to qualify as a business transaction it does not have to be restricted to the buying and selling of *goods* alone. The performance of various services forms one aspect of many transactions, *e.g.* a ride on a bus; the extraction of a tooth; the services given by public utility corporations such as gas, electricity and water; the service offered by an advertising agency and so on. For each of these services *a price must be paid* to complete the transaction. In all of these transactions involving services, the twin elements of *giving* and *receiving* must be present.

6. Recording transactions. We now know that the method by which business transactions are recorded almost universally is by double-entry book-keeping. Basically, most firms still use the system today even though in the bigger business units machines and computers have largely taken over. It must be understood, however, that business machines and computers are merely *tools* for dealing with information more speedily than can be done by hand. Before these sophisticated machines are capable of producing answers the basic information has to be fed into them and this generally means that a human being has to assemble the various items which have to be "processed," as it is called, from whatever sources are available.

At this stage it should be pointed out that where computers or systems of mechanised accounting are in operation the difference between these and the old-fashioned "full set of books" is simply one of method. After all, people used to travel from one place to another by horse-drawn transport. Methods of transportation change with the times but people still travel. In exactly the same way a business needs to record its transactions so that certain conclusions may be drawn; the *method* by which it does so is less important than the fact that it still remains necessary to keep records.

No matter what particular method of recording is in use in a business it is certain that it will be based upon the old art of double-entry book-keeping. From this it follows that a proper understanding of the principles of double-entry book-keeping is essential for anyone who proposes to acquire a knowledge of accounting and to equip himself to use that knowledge.

ORIGINAL DOCUMENTS

7. Sources of information. Before a person can start to record a series of business transactions he must have information. Almost all this information is obtained from *documents, i.e.* pieces of paper with specially designed rulings whereby information of a particular nature can be entered *swiftly and concisely.*

8. Documents in most general use. At this point it is intended only to refer to those documents which are most commonly used so that a student with no business knowledge will be able to envisage from what *source* a particular item of information is obtained.

9. Invoices. An invoice is a document issued by a supplier of goods or of services, *e.g.* electricity, to his customer giving the following information:

(*a*) the date of the transaction,

(*b*) brief details of the goods supplied or service performed,

(*c*) the amount of money involved.

Invoices are usually sent to a customer at the same time, or shortly after the goods are sent to him. Sometimes they accompany the goods.

INVOICE

J. SNODGRASS
Dealer in electrical goods

10, HIGH STREET,
DATE: 2.8.–2   LOWTOWN.

CUSTOMER: D. PERKINS AND SON,
53 MARKET STREET,
WEST WOOD.

INVOICE No. 2785

Quantity	Goods	Price	Amount
12	Electric irons	£2·25	£27·00

NOTE: Invoices are of two kinds:

(*i*) purchase invoices,

(*ii*) sales invoices.

When goods are *purchased* the supplier sends a "sales invoice" to the customer. This will be of the type illustrated above. He will keep *a carbon copy* of the details. This will normally be typed on a "flimsy:" a thin sheet of paper which is placed beneath the customer's invoice.

When the *purchaser* (customer) receives the invoice he calls it a "purchase invoice." The seller retains the "flimsy." He refers to this as a "copy invoice," *i.e.* a "*sales* invoice." From this we can see that *the same invoice* will be regarded differently according to the position of the parties, *i.e.* whether the person concerned is the buyer or the seller.

10. Credit notes. The object of a credit note is to cancel entirely or in part the information shown in an invoice. It is thus a type of "*negative* invoice" and the need to use it arises when, for example, the goods delivered were not the kind ordered. There can, of course, be various reasons for it becoming necessary to issue a credit note but these need not concern us here.

CREDIT NOTE

J. SNODGRASS
Dealer in electrical goods

10, HIGH STREET,
DATE: 5.8.–2   LOWTOWN.

CUSTOMER: D. PERKINS AND SON,
　　　　　　53 MARKET STREET,
　　　　　　WEST WOOD.

CREDIT NOTE No. 64

Quantity	Goods	Price	Amount
1	Electric iron	£2·25	£2·25

Credit notes are always printed in *red* so that they will not be confused with invoices.

11. Monthly statements. Once every month as a rule a supplier of goods sends a summary of the *previous* month's transactions to each of his customers. The customer is thus enabled to check each invoice with the information set out on the summary. This summary is called a "statement."

STATEMENT

J. SNODGRASS
Dealer in electrical goods

10, HIGH STREET,
DATE: 3.9.–2   LOWTOWN.

CUSTOMER: D. PERKINS AND SON,
          53 MARKET STREET,
          WEST WOOD.

Goods supplied for month of August, 1972

Date	Invoice No.	Amount
19–2		
Aug. 2	2785	£27·00
,, 5	C/N 64	2·25
		£24·75

12. Cheques. The settlement of indebtedness between two people or two businesses is largely done by means of payment by cheque. When a person opens an account with a bank he entrusts a certain sum of money to the care of the banker, the understanding being that when he instructs the banker to pay a bill on his behalf he, the banker, will do so. The sum so paid will be deducted by the banker from the original amount with which the account was opened.

In such cases the documents used are called "cheques." The instructions given to the banker are clear and are as follows:

    (*a*) the *date* on which the cheque is "drawn," *i.e.* written out;

    (*b*) the *name* of the person to whom payment is to be made —he is called the "payee";

    (*c*) the *amount* of the payment to be written *in words*;

(*d*) the *amount* of the payment written in *figures*;

(*e*) the cheque must then be *signed* by the person who is entitled to instruct the banker to make the payment, *i.e.* the person whose money the banker is taking care of. This person is called the "drawer."

When a cheque, properly "drawn," is "presented" to the banker for payment the banker will act on those instructions.

CHEQUE

WESTLAND BANK LTD.
58 HIGH STREET
LOWTOWN

Date 4.9.–2

PAY   J. Snodgrass   or Order

Twenty four pounds 75   £24·75

P. Cleghorn
for D. PERKINS & SON

---

13. Petty cash vouchers. Not all payments are made by cheque. Small payments have to be made fairly frequently in most businesses. Postage stamps, small items of office stationery, window cleaning and so on will normally be paid for in cash. Each such payment should have supporting evidence in the form of a document. These documents are usually on a standard office form called "petty cash vouchers," unless some kind of an invoice is produced signed by the person selling the goods.

PETTY CASH VOUCHER

Date 6.8.–2		
	Ink	£0·15
	Stationery	1·20
		£1·35

ACCOUNTING ABBREVIATIONS
AND TERMINOLOGY

14. Some accounting abbreviations. The following are some of the more common accounting abbreviations many of which appear in this book.

A/c	Account	N.L.	Nominal Ledger
b/d	brought down	P.C.B.	Petty Cash Book
b/f	brought forward	P.D.B.	Purchase Day
B/L	Bought Ledger		Book
B/S	Balance Sheet	P.L.	Private Ledger
C.B.	Cash Book	P. & L. A/c	Profit and Loss
c/d	carried down		Account
c/f	carried forward	P.R.B.	Purchase Returns
C/N	Credit Note		Book
Cr	Credit or Creditor	S.D.B.	Sales Day Book
Dr	Debit or Debtor	S.L.	Sales Ledger
e.g.	for example	S.R.B.	Sales Returns
Fol.	Folio or page		Book
i.e.	that is	T.B.	Trial Balance
Inv.	Invoice	Viz.	Namely
Memo.	Memorandum		

15. Accounting terminology.

(*a*) *Casting* or *casting-up*. Adding up a column of figures.

(*b*) *Cross-casting*. Where the items contained in a column of figures have been extended horizontally into a number of analysis columns to the right (or possibly to the left) of the total column, each of the analysis columns should be cast up and the total inserted at the bottom. When the totals of these individual columns are added *across the page* the total of these additions should agree with that of the total column.

(*c*) *Nominal Accounts*. This derives from the Latin word *nomen* meaning "a name." The term "Nominal Account" is used when referring to those expense accounts which bear the name of the particular expense, *e.g.* Salaries, Rent, etc. The term is also used when referring to those few accounts which provide income or profit, *e.g.* Sales, Commission Receivable, etc.

(*d*) *Personal Accounts*. The Latin word *persona* meaning "a person" is the root, hence Personal Accounts, *i.e.* the accounts of persons or firms.

(e) *Real Accounts.* Again, this term comes from the Latin word *res* which means "a thing." Real Accounts deal with things, *e.g.* machines, buildings, shop fittings, motor vehicles, etc.

(f) *Posting.* This means *completing the double entry* of a transaction, one entry of which has already been made. It is also used to make *both* debit *and* credit entries which a transaction requires.

(g) *Sales of goods.* When goods are sold to customers they quite obviously form part of the "sales" for the trading period and will be credited to a "Sales Account." The full name of this account is "Sales of Goods Account" but this title is not used in practice.

(h) *Purchase of goods.* These are debited to the "Purchases Account." It must be understood that this account deals only with the purchase of goods for resale.

PROGRESS TEST 1

Theory

1. What are the fundamental requirements of a business transaction? (2)

2. Each transaction has two aspects. What are they? (4)

3. What is the name of the basic method generally employed for recording business transactions? (5)

4. Name and describe the main sources of information whereby business records may be kept. (6–12)

CHAPTER II

INVESTING IN A BUSINESS

INTRODUCTION

1. The meaning of "accounting." The word "account" has several meanings. We speak, for example, of a newspaperman writing *an account, i.e.* a description, of a certain event; or of a person being asked by the police *to account for* his movements, *i.e.* to state where he was or what he was doing, at a certain time on a certain day. In the Bible we read of a rich man's steward being told to *"render an account of his stewardship"* during his master's absence. In each of these examples the person concerned is *supplying information* in some detail to other people.

In this book we will be using the words "account" or "accounting" in a strictly limited sense, *i.e.* in their relation to money matters. We will be describing the technique of *recording* business dealings in an *orderly and logical fashion* so that certain useful *information* may be extracted from such records.

2. The reasoning underlying the special method employed. It is of vital importance that the beginner should understand *the reasons why* certain things are done in the recording of business transactions. If he passes on to a later stage without fully understanding these reasons, a disastrous gap will be left in his knowledge and he will therefore be incapable of *logically* reasoning out a solution to a problem. This deficiency in his knowledge will greatly diminish his competence and make examination success problematical.

3. The need to keep records. The primary reason why most people go into business is to make money. There may well be a secondary motive, for example where an art-dealer gains considerable pleasure from the handling of good paintings, but motives such as these are usually only incidental to the main object which is for the person concerned to make as good a living as he may from his chosen occupation.

In order to know how much money, or how much *profit*, he has made within a given period it is necessary for him to keep *a record* of all his business transactions: it is very unwise to rely upon memory. If, therefore, the details of each transaction are *written down* at the time they occur a record of a semi-permanent nature at the very least will have been established to which reference may be made at any time in the future.

4. Measuring the profit. At its simplest, profit may be calculated by comparing the amount of money a person has *at the beginning* of a period of trading with the amount he has *at the end* of the period.

EXAMPLE

Smith has £10 which he spends on the purchase of fruit. He calls at numerous houses during the day and by the evening has sold all the fruit for £15.

We can show the result of his business venture in the form of a statement:

Sale of fruit		£15
Less Cost of fruit		10
Profit	=	£5

This simple example gives a clear indication that if there is an *increase* in a person's supply of money *as a result of trading* a profit will have been made.

ACCOUNT SHEETS AND THE LEDGER

5. The account sheet. Business transactions are recorded on sheets of paper called "account sheets." These sheets are ruled in a certain way so that information may be entered conveniently. In the first place a *vertical* line is ruled *down the centre* of the sheet thus dividing it into two halves.

The *left side* is always referred to as the *debit* side and the *right side* is always known as the *credit* side. These are usually shortened to read "Dr" and "Cr."

Further rulings are found on each side of the sheet to facili-

tate the entry of information. The *rulings* of an account sheet
and the *headings* of the various columns are as follows:

Left or debit side (Dr)				Right or credit side (Cr)			
Date	Details	Folio	£	Date	Details	Folio	£

It should be noted that the headings of the various columns
on the *debit* side are *exactly the same* as those on the *credit* side.
The columns headed "Folio" are used for the purpose of
cross-referencing, the word *folio* meaning "*page*." Thus we
must enter in the folio column the reference number of the
account sheet in which *the other part of the double entry* will be
found, for we must not forget that every transaction has two
aspects, one of *giving* and the other of *receiving*.

6. The ledger. As a business may be expected to have a great
many transactions during a period of trading it follows that *a
considerable number of account sheets* will be needed. To avoid
mislaying or losing these sheets as well as for other matters of
convenience we bind them together in the form of a book which
we call the *ledger*.

The information which *must* be entered in the ledger for *each
transaction* is:

    (*a*) the *date* upon which the transaction took place;
    (*b*) very brief *details* regarding the nature of the trans-
action;
    (*c*) the *amount* of money involved.

7. The basic rule of book-keeping. Because every transaction
has *two aspects* and because *both* of these aspects must be
recorded in the appropriate account sheets we can now lay
down the basic rule of book-keeping. The importance of this
rule cannot be over-emphasised since it is the corner-stone upon
which accounting theory and practice is built. The rule is:

    Every *debit entry* in the ledger must have *a corresponding
credit entry*, and every *credit entry* in the ledger must have
a corresponding debit entry.

8. Using account sheets. An account sheet will be used for every different *type* of transaction. If, for example, we wish to record the purchase of a motor van for a business we must open an account sheet in the ledger headed "Motor Van Account." Particulars of the transaction, *i.e.* the date, brief details and the cost of the van, will have to be entered in this "account" (short for "account sheet"), and in the folio column a cross-reference will be entered indicating where we may expect to find *the other half* of the double entry.

When the two halves of a double entry are made this is called "posting the entries."

DEBTOR AND CREDITOR

9. Terms used in accounting. In book-keeping and account-ing, students find that a number of somewhat unfamiliar words or phrases are in common use. It will be found that these expressions become, in a very short time, part and parcel of their vocabulary. (Reference should be made to I, **14** and **15**.) At this stage it is vitally important that the student under-stands the meaning of two of these words, namely, "debtor" and "creditor."

10. The derivation and meaning of the word "debtor." The word "debtor" comes to us from the Latin verb *debeo* which means "I owe." From this Latin word the term "debtor" is derived and it is not difficult to conclude, quite correctly, that a debtor is an "ower," *i.e.* a person who owes something of value *to someone else*. In business, if a person sells goods to a customer for a certain price the customer may, *by arrangement*, pay for those goods at a later date. We therefore say that "a debt has been incurred." The customer, *so long as he has not paid for the goods*, is called a *debtor*.

11. The derivation and meaning of the word "creditor." Once again, it is Latin which provides us with the term "creditor." The Latin verb *credo* has the basic meaning of "I believe." We need to extend that definition a little further in order to see more clearly how it ties in with accounting terminology.

The dictionaries give two meanings, the first of these being

"I trust" or "I have trust in." The second meaning is given as "I have faith in."

If we apply either of these two meanings, for example, to the case of a person borrowing money from someone else, we would say that *the lender* of the money "trusted" or "had faith in" *the borrower, i.e.* he was confident that his loan would be repaid in due course. As a result, the *lender* is referred to as a *creditor*.

THE IDENTITY OF A BUSINESS

12. Bringing a business into existence. It is usually interesting to walk through the busy shopping-centre of any town and look at the shops and stores alive with activity. It is also interesting to contemplate *how* these businesses came into existence. They did not just happen. They are the result of past human endeavour which almost certainly entailed personal sacrifice on the part of the founder such as giving up leisure time in order to master a skill or doing without luxuries so that money might be saved more quickly.

13. The owner and the business. It is of the utmost importance for the student to understand that the business, on the one hand, and the owner of the business, on the other hand, are to be regarded as though they were *two completely separate and independent beings.* The business, in other words, is regarded as having *a life of its own.* This convention is often spoken of as "the entity concept."

Human agency is required to bring a business into existence since, quite obviously, it cannot come into being of its own accord. Once created, however, it is regarded as having an *identity* of its own and is therefore capable of entering into transactions with other people *on its own account.* At the outset a business possesses absolutely nothing and must look to its founder to provide the necessary finance from which it can purchase those assets which it needs. In the light of the "entity concept" it is not difficult to envisage the business and its founder entering into the basic transaction of the latter providing the business with its first asset, *i.e.* a certain amount of money.

14. The ledger is the record of the business. Before we consider recording any transactions there is one important point which must be borne in mind. In the ledger we record the transactions into which *the business* has entered. Personal transactions of the owner outside the business are *not* recorded in the ledger. These are his *private* concern. From this it follows that *every* entry in the ledger is recorded from the viewpoint of *the business* and not from that of the owner.

CAPITAL

15. The nature of capital. The one essential requirement *to start* a business is *money*. Since the business does not yet exist (and is still only a plan in the mind) *the money* which will be so vital to it must be provided by *the creator* of the business. The money so provided is called *capital*. This capital belongs to *the owner*, who *lends it* to the business: it is his *investment* in the business.

We have already seen in **11** above that a person who *lends* money to somebody else becomes that person's *creditor*. We may therefore conclude, quite correctly, that if the owner lends *his* money to a business which he is in the process of creating he must be regarded as a creditor of that business. (Remember that the word *credo* means "I have faith in.") As a creditor of the business the owner has faith in the prospects of the business otherwise he would surely not risk losing his money.

16. The business and the money invested in it. Money, *by itself*, has no particular value. It is only of use when it can be *exchanged* for goods or services which are required by the person who owns the money. Money would be of little value to a man sitting on a raft in the middle of the Atlantic Ocean or to a man lost in the Sahara Desert with no water.

The money which the owner *invests* in the business is not made available merely for it to lay dormant. It is handed over with the intention that certain necessary *preliminary expenses* be met. A business must, first of all, have a place from which it can carry on its trade and so it follows that arrangements must be made to buy or to rent premises. The next logical step is to equip the premises in a manner suited to the needs of the proposed business. For instance, a counter, some shelves, scales and a showcase or two might be regarded as basic requirements, and so these would have to be bought. Then, and most important, a supply of goods to offer for sale to customers must be purchased. All of these things obviously require money for them to be bought and this is how most of *the invested money* is spent.

THE CAPITAL ACCOUNT

17. The nature of the Capital Account. Let us suppose that John Snodgrass has savings amounting to £2,000 and that he proposes to invest it all in a business which he is going to call "The Corner Shop." That is to say he is going to *lend* the money, which belongs to him personally, to this new business which he is planning *to create*. Since "The Corner Shop" is not going to give him anything in return for this loan Snodgrass will have to be regarded as **a creditor** of the business. So, in order to record this situation in the ledger of "The Corner Shop," we will have to open an account sheet headed "Capital Account—John Snodgrass" and on *the credit side* thereof enter the sum of £2,000.

The "Capital Account" in any business is the *personal account* of the *owner* and in it will be recorded all those transactions in which the owner and the business are directly concerned. Thus, if the owner takes money *out of* the business for his *private* use this must be entered in the Capital Account. If, on the other hand, he invests more money in the business this too must be recorded in the Capital Account.

18. The financial relationship between business and owner. In the previous section we said that Snodgrass was going to *lend* £2,000 to the business. It must be understood that this is a very special kind of loan in that *it will not be repaid* until he either closes down the business or sells it. The relationship of the business and the owner is thus unique since if anybody else were to lend money to the business he would expect repayment of his loan *within a reasonable time*. In addition, the lender would not, in normal circumstances, lend money unless he were to receive a reward in the form of "interest" each year. The owner, on the other hand, does not invest (*i.e.* lend) his money under any such agreement. He expects to have to work, probably quite hard, in the business and take *his* reward for both his investment and his work *in the shape of any profits* which the business may make.

The *opening* ledger entries on the creation of "The Corner Shop" would be as follows:

Dr	Capital Account—John Snodgrass	Cr
	Cash Invested in Business A/c	£2,000

Dr	Cash Invested in Business Account	Cr
Capital A/c— John Snodgrass £2,000		

NOTE. In the ledger entries recording the *opening* transaction we have used the abbreviation "A/c" instead of the word "Account." This is the usual practice and in future the abbreviation will be used.

THE BALANCE SHEET

19. The contents of the balance sheet. Now that we have made what are called the *"opening entries"* in the ledger of the business it is a suitable moment to introduce a "statement" which sets out the *position* of the business at this particular moment. This statement is called "the balance sheet" and in it there will be entered:

(a) all those things which the business **possesses**, *i.e.* owns, and

(b) the various amounts of money which the business **owes** to people.

It will be found that the total of (a) will always amount *exactly* to the total of (b). In other words the two totals will "balance," *i.e.* they will be *identical*. Hence this statement is given the title of "the balance sheet." If these two totals do *not* agree this gives us warning that a mistake has been made somewhere. From the *double* entry set out above we can now construct the *opening* balance sheet of John Snodgrass's business, "The Corner Shop."

BALANCE SHEET OF "THE CORNER SHOP"

Amounts owing by the business:

Capital Account—John Snodgrass   £2,000

Things possessed by the business:

Cash invested in the business   £2,000

The above balance sheet has been shown here as a *statement*
and the entries therein have not been referred to as either
"debits" or "credits."

20. The balance sheet and the ledger. This statement, or
balance sheet, is *not* part of the system of double-entry book-
keeping. That is to say, it is *not* an account sheet which will be
found in the ledger. It is constructed *from* entries which have
already been made in the ledger, *i.e.* transactions which in
themselves have been *doubly entered* in the account sheets
appropriate to the circumstances.

NOTE. The beginner must understand that he should never, in
any circumstances, try to *make transfers to* the balance sheet.
The double-entry system confines all entries, both debit and
credit, to the account sheets in the Ledger. Since the balance
sheet is *not* an account sheet in the ledger any attempt to transfer an item from the ledger to the balance sheet is fundamentally
wrong and, technically, an impossibility.

This warning is given because sometimes one finds students
trying to do this.

LIABILITIES AND ASSETS

In the balance sheet (or, as it is sometimes called, the
"statement of affairs") shown in **19** we have used two distinct
headings, *i.e.* "Amounts *owing by* the business" and "Things
possessed by the business." These are somewhat unwieldy
expressions and are not used in practice. Instead, these terms
are referred to as "liabilities" and "assets" respectively.

21. Liabilities. As stated above, when we speak of "liabilities" we mean amounts of money owing *by* the business *to*

somebody else. Hence, if a business acquires something of value, from somebody *without paying for it* (or giving value in return), the business is said to be *liable* for the amount of the debt. The other person is said to be a **creditor** of the business.

It has already been pointed out that a lender must have had *faith* in the business to allow it the use of his money or his goods. If he did not expect that the business would *repay* him in due course it is most unlikely that he would have given it anything of value in the first place. Hence, he is called a "creditor" (from the Latin *credo* meaning "I trust or have faith in"). We shall see later on that *every item* which appears on the "liabilities" side of any balance sheet is a *creditor* of one type or another.

22. The assets of a business. Assets are those things of value which belong to a business. The word "asset" appears to have its roots in the French word *assez* which means *"enough"* or *"sufficiency."* In the context of accountancy *assets should always be equal to liabilities*; that is to say, the business should have enough possessions to satisfy the claims of the creditors (liabilities). In **19** above we saw that the business possessed £2,000 in cash which was just enough to satisfy the claim of the owner (also £2,000).

THE BANKER AND THE BUSINESS

23. Looking after the cash invested in a business. When any business is started it is necessary that a comparatively large sum of money be invested in it for the purposes explained in **16**. All this money will not normally be spent immediately. It takes time to get matters organised and therefore it would be very unwise for the cash to be left lying around. The obvious course would be to put it in a place of safety. This is a job for the specialist. Fortunately, there are certain businesses which specialise in looking after other people's money. These specialist businesses are called *banks* and they have local branches in most towns.

The owner of the new business will therefore take his money to a *banker* who can be trusted to look after it for him. In England there are a number of very large banks, two of which still bear the names of their founders, *i.e.* Barclays Bank and Lloyds Bank.

Let us suppose that John Snodgrass decides to ask Mr. Barclay (of Barclays Bank) to look after the £2,000 which he proposes to invest in his projected business. After going through the preliminary formalities he hands the money over to Mr. Barclay and is given a book of *cheques*. Each cheque bears the instruction "Pay" as its first word. John Snodgrass, from time to time, will, by means of these cheques, instruct Mr. Barclay to pay, from the £2,000 in his possession, certain sums of money to various people for goods received or services rendered.

Before that point is reached, however, let us see what the position would be immediately after the account has been opened at Barclays Bank.

EXAMPLE

Using the details in **17** we will now hand the £2,000 invested in the business to Barclays Bank.

Dr	Capital Account—John Snodgrass	Cr
	Cash Invested in Business A/c	£2,000

Dr	Cash Invested in Business Account			Cr
Capital A/c—John Snodgrass	£2,000	Barclays Bank A/c	£2,000
	£2,000		£2,000

Dr	Barclays Bank Account	Cr
Cash Invested in Business A/c	£2,000	

The balance sheet of the business will now appear as follows:

BALANCE SHEET OF "THE CORNER SHOP"

Liabilities—money that the business owes to people

Capital Account—John Snodgrass	£2,000

Assets—money (or other goods) owned by the business

Bank Account—Mr. Barclay	£2,000

We have now produced a balance sheet which shows the business as being *involved with two persons*. On the one hand, John Snodgrass is a **creditor** of the business, while on the other hand Mr. Barclay is a **debtor** of the business.

24. The balance sheet in debit/credit form. The balance sheet shown in the example in **23** was in the form of *a statement* which set out the situation of the business at a particular moment in time. It was not shown in debit/credit form but in what is known as *"vertical* presentation." If we wished we could set it out as having two separate sides.

BALANCE SHEET OF "THE CORNER SHOP"

Assets (or debit balances)	*Liabilities* (or credit balances)
Bank Account—	Capital Account—
Mr. Barclay	John Snodgrass
(the banker) £2,000	£2,000

25. The balance sheet in traditional form. Strange as it may seem the English form of balance sheet is *not* set out as shown above but with *the assets* appearing *on the right* side and *the liabilities on the left*. Why this should be so is not clear but it is the *traditional* English presentation. If this form is used the balance sheet would be shown as follows:

BALANCE SHEET OF "THE CORNER SHOP"

Liabilities (credit balances)	*Assets* (debit balances)
Capital Account—	Bank Account—
John Snodgrass £2,000	Mr. Barclay £2,000

There is no doubt at all that this is a source of confusion to beginners and for the present we will show all balance sheets in the *vertical* form, *i.e.* as *a statement* set out in the manner shown in the example in **19**.

PROGRESS TEST 2

Theory

1. What do you understand by the term "book-keeping"? **(1)**
2. Why is it necessary to keep records? **(3, 4)**
3. Describe an "account sheet." What is it used for? **(5)**

4. "Account sheets" are bound together to form a book. What information will be found in this book? (6)

5. State the basic rules of double-entry book-keeping. (7)

6. What is a "debtor"? How did the word find its way into our language? (10)

7. State the meaning and derivation of the word "creditor." (11)

8. What is the relationship between a business and its owner? (12, 13)

9. Name the book generally used by businesses to record their transactions. (14)

10. What do you understand by the term "capital"? (15)

11. Why is capital essential to start a business? (16)

12. Explain the purpose of a balance sheet. (19)

13. Explain what liabilities and assets are. (21, 22)

14. Who looks after the money invested in a business? (23)

Practice*

15. M. Lomax set aside £3,000 from his private means for the purpose of starting up a new business to be called "Lomax Motors." An account in the name of the firm was opened with Boyds Bank and the money was paid into it.

Open the necessary accounts in the ledger of the business and record the transactions. Prepare a balance sheet showing the position of "Lomax Motors."

16. R. Ferguson had saved up £4,000 over a number of years. He decided to open a fish-and-chip shop and invested £3,250 of his savings in it. This money was paid into an account at the Redland Bank under the name of "Fergie's Fish Bar."

Open the ledger accounts to record the position and prepare the balance sheet of "Fergie's Fish Bar."

17. N. Bridge won £6,000 in a football pool and as a result decided to fulfil an ambition of his and set up in business on his own account as a greengrocer. Accordingly, he transferred £4,000 of his winnings into an account at the Southern Bank in the name of the business which he called "The Fruit Shop." He discovered later that the business required a further £800 capital so he duly transferred this sum from his private funds.

Open the ledger accounts and enter the above transactions and then prepare the balance sheet of the "The Fruit Shop."

* Suggested answers to these test questions may be found in Appendix II.

CHAPTER III

PREPARING TO TRADE

1. The need for more account sheets. We saw in the last chapter that *money* is the essential requirement to start a business; hence, at the start, the owner *invests* the minimum sum which he estimates the business will need. The money, of course, will be used to buy certain basic equipment together with a reasonable stock of goods to sell to future customers. In addition, some of the money must be retained to meet day-to-day expenses and to provide a fund of small change. This fund is referred to as a "cash float."

With these fresh transactions being entered into it will be necessary to open a number of *extra* account sheets in order to record the details. These sheets will be found in the ledger as discussed in II, 6. It must be emphasised that there is *no limit* to the number of account sheets which may be used by a business. Whenever the necessity arises a new account sheet should be opened.

THE OPENING BALANCE SHEET

2. The basis for all subsequent entries. Once a business has been brought into existence it will continue, in normal circumstances, to exist for an indefinite period. We saw in the last chapter what may be described as "the *opening* balance sheet" of "The Corner Shop," the firm which John Snodgrass created. It is usual to speak of the balance sheet as being the "foundation" upon which all of the book-keeping entries which will follow in the *next* business period must be made. This statement should not be misunderstood. It is simply a way of expressing a mental picture, in a condensed form, of all those ledger balances which go to make up the balance sheet. The important point to be appreciated is that it is *the balances in the ledger* which are gathered together and so, *collectively*, form the statement which we call the "balance sheet."

From this it follows that we must always make absolutely

certain that those balances which appeared in the balance sheet are standing as *"opening"* *balances* in the ledger. If we make sure that this is the case we will know for certain that our ledger does, in fact, *balance,* *i.e.* the *total* of all the debit balances is equal to the *total* of all the credit balances. With the ledger being "in balance" it does not require much imagination to see that if we give *double-entry* effect to the *first* transaction of the new period the ledger will still remain "in balance" *after* these entries have been made. After the *second* transaction has been doubly entered the ledger will still remain "in balance." This pattern, if repeated correctly throughout the whole of this following trading period can therefore have only one result: the ledger will *always* remain "in balance."

EXAMPLE

The "opening" balance sheet of "The Corner Shop" was shown at the end of Chapter II. The next transaction it entered into was the purchase of some shop fittings for £320. Payment was made by cheque immediately and the fittings were installed in a shop which a friend was allowing Snodgrass to use rent-free for six months.

Stage 1. Before we enter the purchase of the shop fittings we will repeat the Capital Account and Bank Account entries which appeared in the previous Example as a reminder. We may safely ignore the "Cash Invested in Business Account" because this was closed off and is no longer of any interest.

Dr	*Capital Account—John Snodgrass*		*Cr*
		Barclays Bank A/c	£2,000

Dr	*Barclays Bank Account*		*Cr*
Capital A/c	£2,000		

NOTE: As was mentioned in Chapter II, **20,** these balances are *not* transferred to the balance sheet. The balance sheet is simply a statement setting out any "balances" which are showing on the various account sheets in *the ledger.* The balance sheet does *not* form part of the *double-entry system*:

we might say that its job is to summarise what is left over at a certain date. The double-entry system of book-keeping is used to show both *the giving* and *the receiving* aspect of each transaction by means of entries in the Ledger. As a result some of the accounts inevitably do not "balance out," thus showing the various things which are *owned* by the business and also what sums of money it *owes* to various people at a particular date. Thus the double-entry system produces certain results in the form of "balances" which, *when collected,* can be set out in the form of a balance sheet.

Stage 2. We will now record the purchase of shop fittings at a cost of £320.

Dr		Bank Account		Cr
Cash Invested in Business A/c (per stage 1)	£2,000	Shop Fittings A/c		£320
		Balance carried down		1,680
	£2,000			£2,000
Balance brought down	£1,680			

Dr		Shop Fittings Account	Cr
Bank A/c	£320		

Stage 3. If we now look through our ledger we will find the following balances on the various accounts:

Capital Account—*Cr*	£2,000 per stage 1
Bank Account—*Dr*	£1,680 per stage 2
Shop Fittings Account—*Dr*	£320 per stage 2

NOTE: The debit balance of £2,000 on the Bank Account *at Stage 1* was brought forward to Stage 2 so now we are only concerned with the *latest* balance on that account, *i.e.* the one at Stage 2.

Stage 4. A balance sheet can now be constructed from the details set out in Stage 3.

BALANCE SHEET OF "THE CORNER SHOP"

Liabilities (credit balances)
    Capital Account—John Snodgrass   £2,000
                                                      ══════

Assets (debit balances)
    Bank Account—Mr. Barclay   £1,680
    Shop Fittings Account   320
                                                      ──────
                                                      £2,000
                                                      ══════

3. Conclusions which may be drawn from this example. Three important points emerge from the above example:

(*a*) We began with the *opening* balance sheet, or, to put it more precisely, the *opening balances on the ledger accounts* which *formed* the "opening" balance sheet. We do, however, *as a matter of convenience* generally refer to these ledger balances as the "opening balance sheet" and *we always start off* from this position.

(*b*) Upon this opening position we superimposed a fresh transaction, namely the purchase of shop fittings for £320. This was paid for by cheque with the result that Mr. Barclay owed "The Corner Shop" *less* than had previously been the case. We observe that the *reduction* in the amount owed by Mr. Barclay *was compensated for* by the value of the shop fittings of which "The Corner Shop" had become the owner and, as a result, the assets of "The Corner Shop" *remained at* £2,000.

(*c*) Even though there had been changes in the form and value of the *assets* the Capital Account of John Snodgrass *was not affected*.

It is very important that this point be appreciated. Snodgrass had invested his £2,000 in "The Corner Shop" and this amount was still *owed to him*. The business, on the other hand, was spending the money on items which it needed to equip itself to begin trading. Thus, there is a change in the composition of the assets but *not* in the Capital Account.

ALTERATIONS IN THE CAPITAL ACCOUNT

4. How the credit balance of the Capital Account can change.
That the Capital Account suffers no change when an alteration

in the shape of the assets takes place was demonstrated in the last example. It is, perhaps, appropriate to refer at this point to those matters which *do* alter the amount standing to the credit of the Capital Account.

Broadly speaking, there are *three* circumstances when alteration *must* be made to the Capital Account. These are:

(*a*) When the owner *increases* the amount of his investment in the business. This can be by means of:

(*i*) *investing* more of his own private money in the business, or
(*ii*) *transferring* a private asset such as a motor car *into the ownership* of the business.

If either of these things happens the owner's investment in the business is increased and the appropriate sum will be *added* to his Capital Account. That is another way of saying that his Capital Account will be *credited*. The corresponding *debit* will appear in the Bank Account or in the appropriate asset account, *e.g.* Motor Car Account.

(*b*) When trading takes place it is the practice periodically to ascertain the amount of the profit (or loss) made during the period of trading. Any *profit* made by the business belongs to the owner and is *added to* the owner's original investment and any loss is *subtracted* from it. These matters will be dealt with in more detail in later chapters.

(*c*) If the owner *withdraws* any of his investment the balance on the Capital Account will be reduced, *i.e.* the amount *owed to the owner* by the business will be *less* than it was before. Reduction of his investment will occur when the proprietor:

(*i*) takes money out of the business for his own *private* use, or,
(*ii*) uses goods, which had *originally been purchased for resale* by the business, for his own personal consumption, *e.g.* a grocer taking tea, sugar, butter, etc., for his household's use.

In either case the Capital Account of the proprietor will be *debited*. The corresponding *credit entries* will be made in the Bank Account (or Cash Account) if money is taken and in the Goods for Resale Account if commodities are withdrawn. Withdrawals of either cash or goods for the owner's personal use are always called "drawings" in book-keeping.

EXAMPLE

Now that "The Corner Shop" has had its shop fitted out it purchases goods at a cost of £1,500 which it intends to sell to the public. These goods were paid for by cheque.

As before, the starting point for the new entries will be based on the balance sheet which we prepared at the end of the example in **3**. Students are again reminded that this balance sheet was prepared from the *balances* which were standing on the *ledger accounts* at that time. In this instance the entries will be as follows:

Dr	Bank Account			*Cr*
Balance brought forward (per Stage 2, example 2 above.)	£1,680	Goods for Resale A/c	£1,500	
		Balance carried down	180	
	£1,680			£1,680
Balance brought down	180			

Dr	Goods for Resale Account	*Cr*
Bank Account	£1,500	

The balances on the Capital Account (£2,000) and on the Shop Fittings Account (£320) which appeared on the balance sheet of the example in **3** remain *unchanged*, *i.e.* they are still standing at those figures in their respective *ledger* accounts. A new balance sheet can now be constructed incorporating the latest transaction.

BALANCE SHEET OF "THE CORNER SHOP"

Liabilities (credit balances)
Capital Account—John Snodgrass	£2,000
	£2,000

Assets (debit balances)
Shop Fittings Account	£320
Goods for Resale Account (**Stock**)	1,500
Bank Account—Mr. Barclay	180
	£2,000

If reference is made to **3** we find that the conclusions apply also to this example. In other words they apply in every case where the asset of cash (or cash at bank) is spent on the purchase of an asset of a different nature, and so the *total* of the assets remains unchanged.

5. Withdrawals of cash and goods. We discussed the effect that withdrawals of the proprietor's investment would have on the Capital Account in the previous section. Let us see by means of an example exactly how the accounts concerned would be affected.

EXAMPLE

Before the business of "The Corner Shop" commenced trading John Snodgrass, the owner, received a demand for payment of the general rates on his *private house* in the sum of £45. As he had invested *all* his private resources in the business he was forced to draw a cheque for this amount (£45) *from* the business bank account. At the same time he took goods, which had cost the business £10, for use in his private household.

Once again, our starting-point must be the *last* balance sheet which was made up of the balances standing in the ledger at that time.

Stage 1. We will deal with the two transactions separately starting with the payment of the rates, £45.

Dr	Bank Account			Cr
Balance brought forward (per example in **5**)	£180	**Capital A/c** (for rates on private house) Balance carried down		**£45** 135
	£180			£180
Balance brought down	£135			

Dr	Capital Account—John Snodgrass		Cr
Bank A/c Balance carried down	**£45** 1,955	Balance brought forward (per example in **5**)	£2,000
	£2,000		£2,000
		Balance brought down	£1,955

Stage 2. The goods taken for private use will be dealt with in the following manner:

Dr		Goods for Resale Account		Cr
Balance brought forward (per example in 4)	£1,500	**Capital A/c** (goods taken for private use)		**£10**
		Balance carried down		1,490
	£1,500			£1,500
Balance brought down	£1,490			

Dr		Capital Account—John Snodgrass		Cr
Goods for Resale A/c	**£10**	Balance brought forward (per Stage 1)		£1,955
Balance carried down	1,945			
	£1,955			£1,955
		Balance brought down		£1,945

Stage 3. The latest balance sheet will be as follows:

BALANCE SHEET OF "THE CORNER SHOP"

Liabilities (credit balances)
Capital Account—John Snodgrass:

Cash introduced		£2,000	
Less: Drawings—			
Cash	£45		
Goods	10		
	—		
		55	
			£1,945

Assets (debit balances)

Shop Fittings Account	£320	
Goods for Resale Account (**Stock**)	1,490	
Bank Account—Mr. Barclay	135	
		£1,945

It will be noted that the Capital Account has been shown in some detail in the balance sheet. Although, strictly speaking, it is not necessary to show anything more than the *closing balances* it is customary to set out any *additions to* or *deductions from* the opening balance.

THE ASSETS SIDE OF THE BALANCE SHEET

6. Marshalling the assets. The assets appearing in the balance sheet shown in the previous section have been set out in a particular order. As can be seen, the item "Shop Fittings" has been shown at the top and beneath it follows "Goods for Resale" (or "Stock," as it is more commonly called). The final item is "Cash at Bank."

It is the practice to place assets in a certain order in the balance sheet putting those items which are of a *permanent* nature at the top. These permanent assets are called "fixed assets." Beneath the fixed assets those items of a *less* permanent nature are set out and are spoken of as "current assets."

In the balance sheet shown above, "Shop Fittings" are placed at the top because they are regarded as being of a permanent nature, *i.e.* they are expected to remain in use for *a long time to come* and are therefore classed as *fixed* assets. Goods for resale (or stock), on the other hand, have been purchased in the expectation that they will be *sold* to customers in as short a time as possible. The intention is that *they shall not be retained* as an asset of the business for any great length of time and, because of this, such goods are classified as current assets. "Cash at Bank" comes under the same heading since this is an asset which is constantly changing.

The expression "marshalling the assets" is used to indicate that they are to be placed in a certain order as a matter of discipline. The modern presentation is to show them in what is known as "descending" order, *i.e.* starting with those which would normally be the most difficult to turn into money and finishing with cash in hand. Very occasionally we see the assets placed in "ascending" order, *i.e.* commencing with Cash and finishing with the most unrealisable of the fixed assets, say, Land and Buildings. This style of presentation, however, is rarely seen nowadays.

7. Fixed assets. It is almost impossible to think of any business which does not have to employ fixed assets of some kind in order to conduct its affairs efficiently. Even the

humble kerbside flower-seller has to use a basket or two as well
as jugs or vases to display her merchandise. She does not
throw these away when she has sold all her stock but takes
them away with her for refilling the following day when she
will continue to carry on her business.

There is thus an essential element of *continuity* which
attaches to those particular assets known as fixed assets. They
have been bought in order to fulfil a definite purpose in the
conduct of a business. Without fixed assets appropriate to the
requirements and scale of the concern it would be impossible
for it to operate and make profits. A firm making motor
vehicles, for example, must possess an immense number of
complex machines to be able to produce its finished product.
A haulage concern will require a certain number of lorries and
vans as well as repair and maintenance equipment. A builder
will need to have ladders, scaffolding, cement-mixing machines,
etc., to enable him to carry out his work.

From these examples it is clear that money has to be
invested in fixed assets to enable a business *to earn profits*. It
should also be clear that when money is spent in this way it is
spent with the intention that these assets *will remain in use* for
a considerable time to come. Hence the use of the term "fixed"
in relation to such assets. In most cases there are two criteria
to be applied when deciding if any asset is to be classed as a
fixed asset and both of these criteria must be met. They are:

(*a*) Will the asset help the business to *operate* more
efficiently and *make profits*?

(*b*) Are the assets to be retained *permanently* in the
business?

The most usual headings under which fixed assets appear in
business balance sheets are:

(*a*) Land and buildings.
(*b*) Plant and machinery.
(*c*) Fixtures and fittings.
(*d*) Office furniture and equipment.
(*e*) Motor vehicles.
(*f*) Patents and trademarks.

This list is not to be regarded as complete but is used to show
the beginner the *type* of items referred to as fixed assets.

8. Current assets. This title is given to those assets of a business which are *changing* from day to day *as a result of trading*. If, for instance, we sell some of our stock of goods the total held by us decreases. On the other hand if we receive money in payment for such sales our supply of money increases. When we purchase more goods or pay the wages of an employee the supply of money diminishes. Such assets are called "current assets." The most usual current assets found in balance sheets are:

(a) Stock of goods for resale.

(b) Debtors, *i.e.* persons to whom we have sold goods but for which we have not yet received payment.

(c) Payments made in advance.

(d) Cash at bank.

(e) Cash in hand.

9. Intangible assets. Not infrequently, we meet with certain assets which, because of their nature, pose a degree of difficulty to a beginner with regard to their classification. Experience can be of great help in this matter but that is the one quality which the beginner cannot be expected to possess.

Assets of an *abstract* nature can be divided into two groups:

(a) Intangible assets.

(b) Debit balances (sometimes spoken of as "assets of no value" which, of course, is a contradiction in terms).

Examples of intangible assets are patent rights and goodwill. Patent rights are rights which are capable of being transferred. Thus, a firm may have paid for the right to use a particular process in the course of manufacture for a specified number of years, thus gaining an advantage of some value over trade competitors.

Similarly, if a person acquires an existing business he usually has to pay the seller a certain sum of money *in excess of* the value of the *physical assets* belonging to the business. This excess payment is spoken of as "goodwill."

Neither patent rights nor goodwill are *physical* assets. They have *an intangible quality* but are, none the less, quite definitely *fixed* assets. Sometimes items which are also intangible but which, at the same time, have no *real* value have to appear on the assets side of a balance sheet (for no other reason than that there is nowhere else for them to go). An example of such an item would be where certain expenses had to be incurred at the time a business was brought into existence. Such expenses are often called "preliminary" or "formation" expenses. The expenses were necessarily incurred at the time but would be of no worth if the business were being sold. Unless there is any good reason for not doing so items such as these should be written off out of profits at the first opportunity.

THE LIABILITIES SIDE OF THE BALANCE SHEET

10. Marshalling the liabilities. Having looked at the manner in which the assets of a business are set out in the balance sheet we know that they are grouped under two main headings, the expression "fixed assets" being used to describe those which have some degree of permanence or continuity, while the term "current assets" is applied to those which alter from day to day.

Much the same principles can be, and are, applied to the liabilities side of the balance sheet, although it must be mentioned that the term "fixed liabilities" is not often encountered. One wonders why this should be so, since there seems to be no special reason for not employing it to cover a particular group of liabilities. Very often we meet with liabilities which can truly be regarded as being of a *semipermanent* nature. We could go further and state that they are more fixed than are many assets to which the title "fixed" is given.

11. Which of the liabilities may be regarded as "fixed"? The principal item on the liabilities side of the balance sheet which may be considered to be a *permanent* feature is, of course, the owner's investment in the business, *i.e.* the balance on his Capital Account. This figure consists of the *original sum* he contributed to the business *plus* any of the subsequent profits he decided to leave therein. Naturally enough the amount of the balance on the Capital Account fluctuates from year to year dependent upon the amount of profit made and the sum withdrawn by the owner for his personal use. The bulk of the capital always remains in the business and so we have every justification for speaking of it as a "fixed" liability.

"Long-term" loans obtained by the business from somebody other than the proprietor are another instance of what may be called "fixed" liabilities, since, by their nature, they are unlikely to be repaid in the *near* future.

12. Current liabilities. Like current assets the characteristic of these items is fluidity. That is to say, they are continually changing because their amount depends upon the day-to-day trading movements entered into by the business. As a general rule they fall under the following sub-headings:

(*a*) Trade creditors, *i.e.* amounts owing for goods supplied.

(*b*) Expense creditors, *i.e.* amounts owing for services supplied.

(*c*) Interest on loans which is due but not paid.

(*d*) Bank overdrafts and other "short-term" loans.

13. All liabilities are of a "personal" nature. If the liabilities side of a balance sheet is studied it will be seen that *every single item* appearing thereon represents a sum of money owing to a person or a firm. This can be seen quite easily if we consider the composition of the items which fall under the two groups called "fixed" liabilities and "current" liabilities.

Fixed liabilities are those sums owed to *people* who have either *invested* money (*e.g.* the proprietor) or who have *lent* money to a business. The latter type of person is often referred to as a "loan creditor."

Looking at classifications (*a*) to (*d*) in **12** above, we can see that the amounts involved represent money owing:

(*a*) to people or firms who have supplied goods on credit;

(*b*) to people who have rendered *services* to the business, such as the local electricity board, who have not yet been paid;

(*c*) to the person who has lent the business money for a long period of time, the interest on his loan being the charge for the *use* of his money, and

(*d*) the money which the *banker* lends the business in the shorter term.

14. Summary of principles. In this chapter we have been mainly concerned with two important points of principle.

The first is that the entries in the opening balance sheet are the foundation *upon which every* future *transaction is built.*

The second is that every transaction, no matter what its nature, causes a change in the balance sheet.

These two principles are of such vital importance to a proper understanding of accounting that they need to be impressed upon students at the earliest possible moment. It is suggested, therefore, that you study this chapter with the greatest care and do not press on to the next stage until you feel that you have fully mastered it.

15. An explanation of two common abbreviations. The terms "carried down" and "brought down" frequently puzzle the beginner and a word of explanation at this point may be helpful.

When the end of a period of trading is reached, *e.g.* the last day of the month or the last day of the financial year, it is usual to "balance off" the accounts in the ledger. Normally, the total of one side exceeds the total of the other and the difference, or "balance," is inserted in order to make the smaller total *equal to* that of the larger.

This balance is then entered on the *opposite* side of the same account but *beneath* the totals which are ruled off, *i.e.* the *double*-entry function is performed as the system requires. It is, of course, quite logical that this should be done since the balance represents the amount by which the greater side exceeds the lesser. In other words, the balance is the amount which is "left over" and it must then be taken into the trading period which *follows* and dealt with at some time during that subsequent period.

The following ledger accounts will illustrate the foregoing explanation:

John Snodgrass Account

May	8	Sales A/c	£142	May 25	Bank A/c	£100
	20	Sales A/c	63			
	29	Sales A/c	87			
			£292			£100

It can be seen that the difference between the two sides amounts to £192. This is called the "balance" and it must be entered, firstly, on the credit side in order to make the total of this side of the account equal to the total of the debit side.

These equal totals will then be "ruled off" as shown below and the balance entered on the debit side *beneath* the total, thus *completing the double entry*.

The account in its completed form will appear as follows:

John Snodgrass Account

May 8	Sales A/c	£142	May 25	Bank A/c	£100
20	Sales A/c	63	31	**Balance c/d**	192
29	Sales A/c	87			
		£292			£292
June 1	**Balance b/d**	£192			

A number of items in this account need a little clarification.

(*a*) The difference, or balance, entered **above** the total of the credit side bears the symbol "c/d" against it. This is a short way of saying "carried down." It is *always* placed against the *upper* of the two balancing entries.

(*b*) As can be seen, the lower entry, *i.e.* the one made **beneath** the total of the debit side bears the symbol "b/d" against it. This is an abbreviation for "brought down."

(*c*) The amount of the balance, £192, is the sum which is "left over," *i.e.* still owing, at the end of the month of May. It must, therefore, be carried on into June for settlement later that month.

(*d*) Observe that the balance "c/d" bears the date of the *last* day of the trading period which is now ended, whereas the balance "b/d" is dated on the *first* day of the following trading period.

(*e*) The symbol "c/d" *always* appears above the total on one side while "b/d" *always* appears underneath the total on the opposite side.

Students may find the following *aide-mémoire* useful: people nearly always speak of *carrying* something downstairs and that when the *foot* of the stairs has been reached they say that they have *brought* that something down.

The principles of the foregoing explanation also apply to "c/f," which is used to indicate a balance which is being "carried forward" to a new period, and to "b/f" which means "brought forward."

PROGRESS TEST 3

Theory

1. Explain what the "opening" balance sheet consists of and the reason for its importance. (2)

2. Do we transfer balances to the balance sheet? (2, note)

3. What important conclusions may be drawn from the example in 2? Write them out and check that you know and understand these points.

4. What events can make an alteration to the Capital Account necessary? (4)

5. What entries are necessary to record:

    (a) the withdrawal of money from the business for the owner's personal use?

    (b) the withdrawal of goods for the private use of the owner? (5)

6. Distinguish between fixed assets and current assets giving your reasons for the distinction. (6, 7, 8)

7. Set out two very important principles which have been dealt with in this chapter. (14)

8. What are two common abbreviations used in accounting? (15)

Practice

9. H. Webster is preparing to open his own business investing £5,000 from his savings. He opens a business account with Boyds Bank and pays in the £5,000. Having found suitable premises he paid a year's rent in advance to the landlord amounting to £750. Equipping the shop cost £1,000 and he bought a stock of goods for £3,000.

Open the necessary ledger accounts and post the above transactions thereto. Prepare a balance sheet setting out the position.

NOTE: The rent paid to the landlord will appear as an asset since he is a *debtor* of the business.

10. P. Jennings had £10,000 which he invested in a new business. He paid this money into a business account which he opened at Chalkleys Bank. He purchased shop premises for £5,750 and bought a motor delivery van for £425. Legal costs on the purchase of the shop amounted to £150. Shop fittings cost £600 and he spent £2,300 on a stock of goods. He then found that he had left himself short of money to pay for the installation of central heating in his private house and so drew £500 out of the bank to pay for it.

Open the necessary ledger accounts and post the above transactions thereto. Prepare a balance sheet setting out the position of the business.

NOTE: The legal costs of £150 must be added to the cost of the premises.

CHAPTER IV

THE CASH BOOK

CASH ACCOUNT AND BANK ACCOUNT

1. Cash transactions. In Chapter II we introduced an account which was called "Cash Invested in Business Account." It was used to point out that the business possessed, for the moment at least, an asset of *cash*. This balanced off *the liability* of the business to its owner. The money was paid into a bank for safe keeping immediately and the banker then appeared as a *debtor* of the business. Thus the Cash Invested in Business Account was *closed off* and not used any more.

Because the transactions of many businesses are entered into on the basis of an immediate cash settlement between the parties it now becomes necessary to bring a "Cash Account" into use. To recognise the necessity of this we need only think of the ordinary shops in any town. All their sales almost without exception are for *cash*, *e.g.* the grocer, the tobacconist, the butcher, the baker, the chemist and so on. The money which these traders receive from sales can amount to a considerable sum daily and even though a large part of this will normally be paid into the business Bank Account the probability is that some of it will be *retained* in the business to pay for certain expenses. In order that transactions which involve the movement of cash both in and out of the business be properly recorded we now open an account sheet headed "Cash Account."

2. Recording transactions in cash. When a sale is made for cash the money received will be debited in the Cash Account and credited in the Sales Account in approved double-entry fashion.

EXAMPLE

Arthur Bond trades as a fishmonger. On 1st May his sales for cash amounted to £45. The ledger entries would be:

Cash Account

May 1	Sales A/c	£45		

Sales Account

			May 1	Cash A/c	£45

On the following day, 2nd May, the previous day's takings were paid into the bank and the Cash Account *closed off*.

Cash Account

May 1	Sales A/c	£45	May 2	Bank A/c	£45

Bank Account

May 2	Cash A/c	£45		

Let us now look at another example in which *only a part* of the day's takings are paid into the bank.

EXAMPLE

Charles Brown, a grocer, sold goods for cash on 3rd May amounting to £82. Before banking next morning he retained £48 for the following: £24 to pay his assistants their wages; £3 for wrapping paper, grease-proof paper, bags, etc.; £1 for postage stamps; £2 for cleaning materials and £18 for his own personal and household expenses.

After these various payments have been made the Cash Account would be written up thus:

Cash Account

May 3	Sales A/c	£82	May 4	Wages A/c	£24
				Wrapping	
				Paper A/c	3
				Postages A/c	1
				Cleaning A/c	2
				Capital A/c	
				(drawings)	18
					£48

The normal double entry would be made with respect to each individual item, *i.e.* Sales Account would be credited with £82; Wages Account debited with £24, etc. Finally, the *remainder* would be paid into the bank, the entries being:

Cash Account

May 3	Sales A/c	£82	May 4	Sundry payments as above	£48
				Bank A/c	34
		£82			£82

Bank Account

May 4	Cash A/c	£34

3. Money paid into the Bank Account. It is important for the student to recognise that when money (cash) is *paid into the bank* this must be treated as a payment *out of cash* in precisely the same way as is any other amount which has been paid out. That is to say, so far as the Cash Account is concerned the money has been *disposed of*. It is true, of course, that the money has not been lost to the business as would be the case where it is used to pay for goods or for services rendered, for money once spent cannot be spent again. The money has merely been *moved* to another place and the Cash Account is, so to speak, no longer responsible for it; this is now the responsibility of the banker.

4. Dealing with cash withdrawn from the bank. It is by no means unusual for a firm to need to draw cash out of its Bank Account in order to make certain payments in cash. Many firms follow the rule that *all* cash received shall be paid into the bank *without any deductions*. This is a prudent rule to follow but it is not always adopted by any means. Where it is the rule, it means that cash will have to be drawn out of the bank each week to pay wages, for example. A further amount may be required to meet the day-to-day petty expenses such as fares, postage stamps, etc. In cases such as these a cheque will be drawn (as for any other payment out of the bank) and will be credited in the Bank Account, the corresponding debit being made in the Cash Account.

EXAMPLE

W. Mullins who kept a bakery, drew £32 from the business bank account to pay his assistants' wages. The entries to record this would be:

Bank Account

| | | Cash A/c (for wages) | £32 |

Cash Account

| Bank A/c | £32 | | |

To complete the picture let us record the actual payment of the wages.

Cash Account

| Bank A/c (as above) | £32 | Wages A/c | £32 |

Wages Account

| Cash A/c | £32 | | |

THE TWO-COLUMN CASH BOOK

5. The Cash Account and the Bank Account side by side. A long time ago it was the recognised custom to keep the Cash Account and the Bank Account in a separate book which was regarded as being a part of the ledger. The name given to this separate book was the "Cash Book."

The two accounts in the Cash Book were not kept in the same manner as were those in the ledger. Instead of the two accounts being kept *in different parts* of the Cash Book they were kept *side by side*.

The rulings were as follows:

CASH BOOK

Date	Details	Cash A/c	Bank A/c	Date	Details	Cash A/c	Bank A/c

It is not proposed to enlarge greatly on this matter at this stage because experience has shown that beginners tend to get confused in the operation of the *"two-column* cash book." Later on, when they are more experienced, will be time enough for them to test themselves in its operation. It is a good discipline to master and can be very useful in both examination work as well as in practice but at this early stage it is best avoided. A simple example will suffice for the time being.

EXAMPLE

J. Snodgrass paid £1,500 out of his private assets into a business bank account on 1st May.

May 1	Paid by cheque for shop fittings	£345
2	Purchased goods, paying by cheque	1,000
2	Drew cash from bank by cheque	25
3	Sold goods for cash	21
4	Paid rent by cheque	30
5	Bought stationery and postage stamps for cash	7
6	Sold goods for cash	125
7	Paid wages in cash	12
7	Paid cash into bank	130

If we used a *separate* account for the "bank" transactions we would show the following:

Bank Account

May 1	Capital A/c	£1,500	May 1	Shop Fittings A/c		£345
7	Cash A/c	130	2	Purchases A/c	£1,000	
			2	Cash A/c		25
			4	Rent A/c		30
			7	Balance c/d		230
		£1,630				£1,630
	Balance b/d	£230				

We will now deal with the "cash" transactions in a *separate* account.

Cash Account

May 2	Bank A/c	£25	May 5	Stationery A/c	£7
3	Sales A/c	21	7	Wages A/c	12
6	Sales A/c	125	7	Bank A/c	130
			7	Balance c/d	22
		£171			£171
	Balance b/d	£22			

Having shown the entries in the normal manner let us now present them as in a two-column cash book.

		Cash A/c	Bank A/c			Cash A/c	Bank A/c
May 1	Capital A/c		£1,500	May 1	Shop Fittings A/c		£345
2	Bank A/c	£25		2	Purchases A/c		1,000
3	Sales A/c	21		2	Cash A/c		25
6	Sales A/c	125		4	Rent A/c		30
7	Cash A/c		130	5	Stationery A/c	£7	
				7	Wages A/c	12	
				7	Bank A/c	130	
				7	Balance c/d	22	230
		£171	£1,630			£171	£1,630
	Balance b/d	£22	£230				

Whichever method is used it can be seen that the balances are absolutely identical. This is, of course, what we would expect, since the principles of double-entry book-keeping have been followed in each case.

Beginners are warned to be very cautious when attempting the two-column method and are advised to prepare their answer in the normal, *i.e.* ledger-account, form in the first place. They should then work the problem in the two-column form. If the balances agree with those shown by the normal ledger-account method then it can be accepted that the answer is right. On the other hand if the balances *disagree* then the best thing to do is to check the entries in the ledger-account form with those in the two-column form. This check should show where any error lies.

PROGRESS TEST 4

Theory

1. Why is it necessary for a Cash Account to be used as well as a Bank Account? **(1)**

2. How should sales for cash be recorded? **(2)**

3. When money, which a business has received from customers, is paid into the bank how should this be shown in (*a*) the Cash Account, and (*b*) the Bank Account? **(3)**

4. What do you understand by the term "the two-column cash book"? **(5)**

Practice

5. Record the transactions below in the Bank Account and the Cash Account of J. Kinnear's business and bring down the balances on the respective accounts at 31st March.

Mar. 1	J. Kinnear commenced business with capital—	
	cash at bank	£400
	cash in hand	20
2	He bought goods from R. Moore paying for them by cheque	300
3	He bought goods for cash	18
4	Cashed cheque for office expenses	20
7	Cash sales	63
7	Paid cash into bank	60
12	Sold goods to J. Haynes who paid for them by cheque	150
17	Paid sundry expenses in cash	4
28	Bought goods from R. Moore and paid him by cheque	200
30	Cash sales	35
30	Paid one month's rent by cheque	20
31	Withdrew cash for personal use	30

6. Record the transactions below in the Bank and Cash Accounts of M. Peters and bring down the respective balances at 5th July.

July 1	M. Peters decided to open a shop and on this date he paid £1,000 of his private resources into a business bank account	
2	He paid for shop fittings by cheque	£75
3	He rented a shop paying three months' rent in advance by cheque	120
4	He bought goods from R. Morgan paying by cheque	248

5	Drew a cheque for cash to use in the business	25
6	Peters opened his shop and sold goods for cash	67
8	Bought goods for cash	45
9	Sold goods for cash	37
10	Bought wrapping paper and bags for cash	8
11	Sold goods for cash	64
12	Paid assistant's wages in cash	12
13	Sold goods for cash	44
14	Peters paid cash into the bank	145
15	He drew £30 out of the bank account for his personal use	

CHAPTER V

THE ANALYSED PETTY CASH BOOK

CASH PAYMENTS

1. The need to make payments by cash instead of by cheque.
Businesses normally pay their suppliers by cheque and this
means that each payment is recorded through the Bank
Account in the cash book. Apart from these monthly accounts
there are, however, many small payments which a business has
to make on a day-to-day basis. The nature of these payments
is such that it would be absurd, if not impossible, to attempt to
pay by cheque items such as the following: bus or taxi fares,
postage stamps, small items of stationery, window cleaning,
etc. Consequently, it is necessary to bring into use an additional book known as the "Petty Cash Book." This is an
offshoot of the main cash book.

2. The basic design of the petty cash book. The type of Petty
Cash Book most generally used is designed for convenience. As
with the other sections of the ledger it is based on the principles
of double entry. The lay-out is somewhat unusual when compared with the normal account sheet, however. This can be
seen from the illustration set out below which shows that there
is *one common column* to cover the *description* of items of income
on the one hand and items of expenditure on the other. The
reason for such economy of space is because petty cash
"receipts" are normally so few in number that they do not justify
the occupation of two valuable columns, one of which, for most
of the year, would have nothing recorded in it.

In the illustration below the date column has been omitted
as being comparatively unimportant. We are more concerned
with presenting *the layout of receipts and payments*. With
regard to the position of the date column this can be regarded
as being a "variable" in that some rulings place it on the
extreme left-hand side whereas others place it on the left of the
"Description" column, and on the right of the "Receipts"
column. The *position* of the date column is of no importance.

So long as the date of the transaction is recorded *somewhere* that is all that matters in practice.

Dr		Cr
Receipts	*Description*	*Payments*
£25	Bank A/c	
	Train fares	£3
	Postage stamps	2
	Stationery	5
	Petrol	4
	Wages—cleaner	8
		22
	Balance c/d	3
£25		£25
£3	Balance b/d	

As can be seen the presentation is a little unusual but *the essential debit and credit* columns are there giving the necessary information.

3. Analysing the petty cash book. Owing to the smallness of many petty cash payments the book is extended on the right-hand side and divided into a number of *analysis* columns. The amount of each separate payment is then *repeated* by being itself entered into whichever of the analysis columns is appropriate. Each of these columns is headed individually with a description of the *type* of expense it covers, *e.g.* "Postage and stationery," "Travelling expenses," "Motor expenses," etc.

Because many of these payments *recur*, possibly several times in the course of a month, they are "collected" in the analysis column concerned and at the end of the month (usually) the *total* is posted to the debit of the nominal account in the private ledger. As a result of using this method *only one posting per month* (comprising the numerous small payments) will be necessary.

IMPRESTS

4. The "imprest" system. The imprest system of controlling petty cash expenditure is very widely used. In the first place the cashier will *estimate the maximum amount* he will require in any selected period, *e.g.* a week, a fortnight or a month. He will then draw a "cash" cheque for the total estimated amount and place the sum so drawn from the bank in a petty cash box. This sum of money is called the "petty cash float." The double entry will be made by a credit entry in the Bank Account and a corresponding debit in the "Receipts" column of the petty cash book.

During the selected period the cashier will make payments in cash as and when they become necessary, entering each item in the "Payments" column of the Petty Cash Book, *i.e.* on the credit side. (The corresponding debit entries will be made at the end of each month, in the private ledger but only *in total* as was mentioned in the previous section.)

At the end of the selected period, *e.g.* week, fortnight, etc., the cashier will ascertain the total amount of petty cash *which has been spent.* He will then draw a cheque for this amount thus restoring his petty cash float to its *original figure* with which he can start the following period. This is the essence of the imprest system of controlling petty cash, *i.e. the periodical restoration* of the cash fund to its original figure.

The below example illustrates the manner in which a petty cash book is kept and the operation of the imprest system.

Date	Receipts	Description	Pay-ments	Fares	Postage & stationery	Motor expenses	Wage	Sundries
Jan 1	£50	Bank A/c						
4		Train fares	£3	£3				
8		Postage stamps	2		£2			
11		Stationery	5		5			
12		Petrol	4			£4		
14		Wages—cleaner	8				£8	
15		Van repairs	7			7		
20		Taxi fare	2	2				
23		Petrol	5			5		
28		Wages—cleaner	8				8	
31		Donation	1					£1
			45	£5	£7	£16	£16	£1
		Balance c/d	5					
	£50		£50	P.L.	P.L.	P.L.	P.L.	P.L.
Feb 1	£5	Balance b/d						
1	£45	Bank A/c						

This example covers a period of one month. If the totals of the analysis columns are *cross-cast* it will be seen that they amount to £45, *i.e.* this agrees with the *total* of the "Payments" column. The imprest is *restored* to £50 by the drawing of a "cash" cheque for £45, being the amount of the January expenditure on petty cash items. The letters "P.L." at the foot of each analysis column refer to the "private ledger" to which each total is posted.

5. Verification of the petty cash balance. The imprest system lends itself particularly well to easy control of petty cash. It is based on the principle that if the money has not been spent it should be present physically in the cash box. Conversely, if any of the money *has* been spent there should be supporting petty cash vouchers, duly signed, to account for whatever has been spent. Thus, the *total* of the vouchers plus the amount of cash in hand, *i.e.* physically present, should equal the imprest figure which had been previously agreed between the cashier and the accountant or secretary and officially authorised.

Since petty cash is often given into the charge of a junior member of the cashier's staff the knowledge that the imprest can be so easily verified is bound to act as a "moral" check and dissuade a person from acting dishonestly.

PROGRESS TEST 5

Theory

1. Most businesses make certain payments in cash rather than by cheque. Why is this? **(1)**
2. Show the basic layout of a petty cash book, *i.e.* before the introduction of any analysis columns. **(2)**
3. Describe what benefits may occur to a business through the use of analysis columns. **(3)**
4. What do you understand by the term "The imprest system"? How does it operate? **(4)**
5. Draw up a "pro-forma" analysed petty cash book. **(4)**
6. How would you verify that the amount of cash found in the petty cash box was correct? **(5)**

Practice

7. Design an analysed petty cash book and record the following:

May 1 Received "imprest" of £20
   1 Bought postage stamps, £2
   2 Taxi fare, £1
   2 Donation to charity, £0·50
   3 Purchased loose-leaf ledger and supply sheets of spare paper, £3·50
   4 Bought ink, blotting paper and a supply of ball-point pens, £2·75
   4 Paid for tea, milk and sugar for office use for the week, £2·75
   5 Bought cleaning materials, £0·75
   6 Paid office cleaner's wages, £5
   6 Sundry fares, £0·80

Balance off the petty cash book and carry down the balance. Renew the "imprest" on 8th May.

CHAPTER VI

THE FIRST PERIOD OF TRADING

STARTING BUSINESS

1. Completion of preparations for trading. All of the pre-liminaries which were needed to place the business in a position to *start* trading have now been completed. Let us see what happens when "The Corner Shop" actually engages in business operations.

EXAMPLE

During the first month of trading the following transactions were entered into by "The Corner Shop."

Cash sales to customers during the month	£2,040
Purchases of goods for re-sale (paid for by cheque)	112
Wrapping paper and bags (paid for by cheque)	18
Assistant's wages (paid for in cash)	48
Stationery and business ledger (paid for in cash)	6

All of the goods bought for re-sale, including the stock previously purchased, were sold during the month. The balance of cash at the end of the month was paid into the Bank Account.

Stage 1. Before we begin to deal with any of the trading transactions we must remember that the opening balance sheet must form the foundation of all future entries in the ledger. As we know, this is the same thing as saying that we must start with the balances which appeared in the ledger accounts at the date of the last balance sheet. These ledger balances were:

Capital Account—John Snodgrass

	Balance b/f (per Stage 2, example in III, 5) £1,945

Shop Fittings Account

Balance b/f (per Stage 2, example in III, 2) £320	

Purchase of Goods for Resale Account

Balance b/f (per Stage 2, example in III, 5) £1,490	

Bank Account—Mr. Barclay

Balance b/f (per Stage 1, example in III, 5) £135	

A quick check of the debit balances reveals that they total £1,945. This is also the total of *the one and only* credit balance, *i.e.* the Capital Account of John Snodgrass. We thus satisfy ourselves that the ledger is "in balance" and we may safely proceed to record the transactions of the first month of trading.

Stage 2. The first item we will deal with is the sale of goods to customers for cash. At this point it will be convenient to open an account which deals with *"cash" transactions.* Most of the cash receipts will normally be paid into the bank but one usually finds that certain payments such as weekly wages paid to staff are paid out of cash "takings" *i.e.* sales. As we saw in the last chapter the Cash Account operates in precisely the same way as does the Bank Account, *i.e.* receipts of cash are *debited* therein and any cash payments credited to the account.

Cash Account

Sales A/c (receipts of cash from customers) £2,040	

Sales Account

	Cash A/c £2,040

Stage 3. At some time during the month "The Corner Shop" found that a further supply of goods was required. These were paid for by cheque. We will, therefore, bring forward the Bank Account and the Goods for Resale Account from Stage 1.

Bank Account

Balance b/f (per Stage 1)	£135	**Goods for Resale A/c** Balance c/d	**£112** 23
	£135		£135
Balance b/d	£23		

Goods for Resale Account

Balance b/f (per Stage 1) **Bank A/c**	£1,490 **112**	Balance c/d	£1,602
	£1,602		£1,602
Balance b/d	£1,602		

Stage 4. We must now introduce certain expenses connected with the running of the business. The first of these is the *purchase* of wrapping paper and bags. Here it is necessary to point out the difference of a *purchase* of this nature from that of a *purchase* of goods for resale. The paper and bags are *not* for resale; they are merely regarded as *a necessary expense* which must be set against the profit made when goods are sold. The expense, in a sense, is incurred for the convenience of the customers. A very necessary convenience, it must be admitted, in most cases.

Some beginners, when they see the word "purchase" or "purchases" immediately conclude that it refers to goods for resale and charge the item, *no matter what its nature*, to the "Purchase of Goods for Resale Account." Needless to say, this is not the correct treatment and this word of warning should be carefully noted.

Bank Account

Balance b/d (per Stage 3)	£23	Wrapping Paper A/c	£18
		Balance c/d	5
	£23		£23
Balance b/d	£5		

Wrapping Paper Account

Bank A/c	£18		

Stage 5. We now come to the two cash payments. These will both be dealt with under this stage since they are of a similar nature.

Cash Account

Balance b/f (per Stage 2)	£2,040	Wages A/c	£48
		Stationery A/c	6
		Balance c/d	1,986
	£2,040		£2,040
Balance b/d	£1,986		

Wages Account

Cash A/c	£48		

Stationery Account

Cash A/c	£6		

Stage 6. The last instruction is that the "balance" of cash at the end of the month is to be paid into the Bank Account.

Cash Account

Balance b/f	£1,986	Bank A/c	£1,986

Bank Account

Balance b/f (per		Balance c/d	£1,991
Stage 4)	£5		
Cash A/c	**1,986**		
	£1,991		£1,991
Balance b/d	£1,991		

THE TRIAL BALANCE

2. An essential check. Before proceeding to ascertain the results of trading we must *always* make a check in order to ensure that the double entry has been properly carried out and that all the additions in the respective accounts have been made correctly. This check is called the "trial balance" and although it has certain limitations (which will be discussed later in XII, 4 and 5) it is basically an excellent device for checking the accuracy of the entries made in the ledger.

Owing to the operation of the double-entry system, *i.e.* of one debit entry and one credit entry for *each* business transaction, the *total* of all the debit entries *must* equal the *total* of all the credit entries if the double entry has been properly carried out. One very important point for the beginner to note is illustrated in the Bank Account shown in **1** above. It is that when an account is "balanced off" in the ledger, the balance is *first of all* entered **above** the "total" rulings on that side of the account which requires it, in order that *the total of that side* is made to *equal* the total of the larger and *opposite* side. The balance is then entered **below** the "total" rulings on the side **opposite** to its original entry. Thus the precept of every debit entry having a corresponding credit entry is maintained. We can thus see that if the *full* double entry is carried out the ledger *must* be in balance. This is what the trial balance will tell us. If the two totals of the trial balance are *not* in agreement we must check through our work in order to find our error.

To return to the example in **1**:

Stage 7. We will now summarise the balances from the various sections in order to see more easily the final balances on the respective accounts. Note that where this system of "stages" is employed showing the gradual build-up of the various accounts we must always use the *last* appearance of a particular account for the purpose of the trial balance. We will therefore begin at the last stage (Stage 6) and work backwards.

Bank Account

Balance (per Stage 6) £1,991	

Note that the Cash Account was eliminated at Stage 6, and is therefore *not required*.

Wages Account

Balance (per Stage 5) £48	

Stationery Account

Balance (per Stage 5) £6	

Wrapping Paper Account

Balance (per Stage 4) £18	

The Bank Account at Stage 4 (and earlier) was carried forward to Stage 6, and therefore any balances appearing at those *earlier* stages are now ignored. The *up-to-date* balance is the one at Stage 6, *i.e.* £1,991.

NOTE: The various "stages" shown here are simply used as a means of teaching and they would *not* be used in practice.

Goods for Resale Account

Balance (per Stage 3) £1,602	

Sales Account

	Balance (per Stage 2) £2,040

Capital Account

	Balance (per Stage 1) £1,945

Shop Fittings Account

Balance (per Stage 1) £320	

We may now extract the trial balance:

TRIAL BALANCE OF "THE CORNER SHOP"

	Debit balances	*Credit balances*
Bank A/c	£1,991	
Wages A/c	48	
Stationery A/c	6	
Wrapping Paper A/c	18	
Goods for Resale A/c	1,602	
Sales A/c		£2,040
Capital A/c		1,945
Shop Fittings A/c	320	
	£3,985	£3,985

Since the *total* of the debit column equals the *total* of the credit column we can feel satisfied that our ledger is correct and so we move on to the preparation of what are known as the "final" accounts.

THE FINAL ACCOUNTS

3. Ascertaining the "gross" trading profit. The first step to be taken in order to ascertain the amount of profit made during a period of trading is to prepare an account which calculates what is called "the gross profit." Gross profit is the *difference* between:

(*a*) the amount for which goods have been *sold*, and
(*b*) the amount which those *same* goods *cost*.

The account used to present this information is known as the "Trading Account." This is the *first* of the final accounts.

In the example in II, **4** we showed that some fruit which had *cost* £10 had realised £15 when *sold*. The difference between the cost price and the selling price was £5. We would call this sum of £5 the "gross" profit. It must be appreciated that for gross profit to be earned the goods *must* have been *sold*. If goods are *not* sold no profit can arise. This matter will be dealt with in greater detail in Chapter VIII.

4. The calculation of the "net" profit on trading. When the gross profit has been determined the last task to be performed is that of compiling a list of the various expenses which have had to be met and then *subtracting the total* of these from the gross profit. The result is called the "net" profit and this is the really important figure, for this sum is the amount which belongs to the owner. *This is what he has been working for.*

Again, we have to maintain the *double* entry as we prepare this, the *second* of the two **final** accounts: the Profit and Loss Account. The various "expense" accounts are *closed off* by means of credit entries, these amounts then being entered on the debit side of the Profit and Loss Account. Picture it as plucking the expense item *out of* its nest and dropping it into this new account: the Profit and Loss Account.

THE CLOSING ENTRIES

5. Summarising the income and expenses. The Trading Account and the Profit and Loss Account, the two **final** accounts, summarise *all of the costs* incurred during a period of trading and *all the income* received.

As has already been stated, in order to produce these "summaries" we still continue to carry out the principles of double entry since these final accounts are a part of the system. When we build up these final accounts all that we are really doing is to *pick up* the particular balance on *each* of the numerous accounts concerned *and place it in one or other of the final accounts*. For example if we refer to Stage 7 we see that there is a credit balance in the Sales Account. This has got to be *moved out* of this account and *moved into* the Trading Account, being entered therein on the *credit* side. To perform the *double* entry we have, therefore, to make a *debit* entry in the Sales Account thus "closing it off."

Stage 7 contains a number of expense accounts and similar treatment must be given to these but in their case the *debit* entries will be made in the *Profit and Loss Account*. The corresponding credits will appear in the respective expense account thus closing them off.

We shall now continue with the example in **2**.

Stage 8. At this point we will make those closing entries necessary for the construction of the Trading Account so that we may see the position at the end of the first month's operations. As its name implies the Trading Account is a ledger account in exactly the same way as are any of the other accounts which we have met. It is, therefore, imperative that the system of *double* entry be maintained when preparing the Trading Account.

Goods for Resale Account

Balance (per Stage 7)	£1,602	**Trading A/c**	£1,602

Sales Account

Trading A/c	£2,040	Balance (per Stage 7)	£2,040

Trading Account

Goods for Resale A/c	£1,602	**Sales A/c**	£2,040
Gross profit (transferred to Profit and Loss A/c)	438		
	£2,040		£2,040

Profit and Loss Account

		Gross profit (transferred from Trading A/c)	£438

Stage 9. We come now to the *second* of the two final accounts: the Profit and Loss Account. Once again, as the name suggests, this account is a *ledger account* and it is constructed on the normal *double-entry* basis. The various day-to-day *expenses* of running the business of "The Corner Shop" will be *debited* to the

Profit and Loss Account, the corresponding credit entries being made in the expense accounts concerned thus *closing off* those accounts.

Wages Account

Balance (per Stage 7)	£48	Profit and Loss A/c	£48

Stationery Account

Balance (per Stage 7)	£6	Profit and Loss A/c	£6

Wrapping Paper Account

Balance (per Stage 7)	£18	Profit and Loss A/c	£18

Profit and Loss Account

Wages A/c	£48	Gross profit transferred	
Stationery A/c	6	from Trading A/c	
Wrapping Paper A/c	18	(per Stage 7)	£438
	72		
Balance c/d	366		
	£438		£438
		Balance b/d	£366

By subtracting the expenses total of £72 from the gross profit we ascertain that the *net profit* amounts to £366.

6. The closing double entry. It will be noted that the Profit and Loss Account set out above has been left in an incomplete state and that a balance has been struck and carried down. The reason for this is to emphasise the logic of the *closing* double entry for the trading period which is dealt with below. "The Corner Shop" is the creation of its owner John

Snodgrass. He conceived the idea of creating his own business; it is he who is risking his private savings; it is he who is giving of his time, his knowledge and his labour in an effort to make a success of the venture. It is reasonable to conclude, therefore, that any profit which the business makes *must belong to the owner*. The *closing* double entry, therefore, will be to debit the Profit and Loss Account with the net profit and to make the corresponding *credit* entry in the Capital Account of John Snodgrass. The effect of this is to increase the amount which "The Corner Shop" owes him.

Profit and Loss Account

Capital A/c—John Snodgrass	**£366**	Balance (per Stage 9)	**£366**

Capital Account—John Snodgrass

Balance (per Stage 7)	£1,945
Profit and Loss A/c (net profit)	366
	£2,311

7. Preparing the balance sheet. At this point we are left with a number of ledger accounts, each with a balance standing to its debit or credit. These will now be collected and placed together in the summary which we call the "balance sheet" (*see* II, 19).

If reference is made to the trial balance at Stage 7 it will be noted that some of the accounts which had balances at the time it was taken out have now been eliminated by virtue of the transfer of these balances to either the Trading Account or the Profit and Loss Account. We are thus left with very few accounts on which any balance stands. For the sake of clarity let us take out a fresh trial balance before preparing the balance sheet. It is not necessary that this should be done, of course, but it may help students to appreciate the overall picture a little better.

Trial Balance

	Debit balances	Credit balances
Bank A/c	£1,991	
Capital A/c—John Snodgrass		£2,311
Shop Fittings A/c	320	
	£2,311	£2,311

The two sides agree and we can safely proceed to the last stage, *i.e.* the preparation of the balance sheet.

BALANCE SHEET OF "THE CORNER SHOP"

Liabilities (credit balances)
Capital Account—John Snodgrass:

Cash introduced			£2,000	
Add: Profit for the period			366	
			2,366	
Less: Drawings:				
Cash	£45			
Goods	10			
	—		55	
				£2,311

Assets (debit balances)

Shop Fittings Account	£320	
Bank Account—Mr. Barclay	1,991	
		£2,311

Attention is again called to the fact that *a considerable amount of detail* is shown in the balance sheet with regard to the Capital Account. As was pointed out in the last chapter it is not strictly necessary to set out this detail but, as a matter of convention, it is usual to do so. It does, of course, have its positive side in that one can see at a glance what might be called the "owner's dealings" with the business.

PROGRESS TEST 6

Theory

1. Why is the "opening" balance sheet regarded as being of great importance? (**1**)
2. What is the purpose of the trial balance? (**2**)

3. Explain what is meant by the term "the final accounts."
(3, 4)

4. What is the "net" profit and how is it ascertained? (4, 5)

5. What is the last double entry to be made at the end of a period of trading? State the reasons for making this particular double entry. (7)

Practice

6. Early in April, S. Leigh decided to invest £3,500 of his own money in a business which he named "The Sports Shop." He paid the money into a bank account which was opened in the name of the business. Leigh then proceeded to equip the shop with glass counters, drawers, shelves and show cases all at a cost of £625. £370 was then spent on lighting, display lamps and the like. As soon as the shop was ready he purchased sports goods and equipment costing £2,360. All payments were made by cheque. By the end of April he was in a position to commence trading.

Open the ledger accounts and record these transactions therein and then prepare an opening balance sheet.

7. S. Leigh opened his sports shop on 1st May and during that month the following transactions were entered into:

May	6	Paid by cheque for advertising	£21
	12	Purchased stationery and account books paying by cheque	15
	17	Bought goods for resale by cheque	63
	22	Paid one month's rent by cheque	50
	26	Paid assistant's wages by cheque	40
	31	Leigh sold his entire stock of goods (including those purchased on 17th May) during the month, for £2,978. This sum was paid into the bank in two amounts, *i.e.* £1,200 on May 16 and £1,778 on May 31.	

Enter the above transactions in the ledger opening fresh accounts where necessary. Take out a trial balance and prepare the final accounts and balance sheet on 31st May.

CHAPTER VII

PROFIT

THE TWO ASPECTS OF PROFIT

1. The abstract aspect of profit. Profit may be described as the reward which becomes due *to the owner* of a business as a result of a successful period of trading. At the start of that period he was owed a certain sum which was shown in the ledger as *a credit balance* on his Capital Account. After the period of trading has been completed the net profit which has resulted is credited to his Capital Account thus *increasing* the original credit balance. In other words *the debt due* to the owner is increased.

We do not need to be told that a "debt" is not something which can be handled. It does not possess physical qualities: it cannot be passed from hand to hand. Nevertheless, it does *exist*. A debt is "enforceable at law" which means that a debtor can be taken to court by his creditor and judgment may be obtained against him, *i.e.* he can be *forced* by law to pay his debt. From this it can be seen that profit (which is a form of debt due to the owner) has an *abstract* quality in that this aspect, although *invisible*, does undoubtedly exist. It appears in the balance sheet as a liability in the form of an *addition* to the capital.

2. The concrete aspect of profit. There is a second aspect to profit and this aspect is a *visible* one. That is to say, it *can* be seen; it *does* possess physical attributes; it *can* be passed from hand to hand. Profit in its *concrete* form takes the shape of *money*.

EXAMPLE

John Snodgrass commences business on 1st July with a capital in cash of £1,000. On that date he paid for a second-hand motor vehicle which had been specially converted to his requirements for a total cost of £600. He then proceeded to trade as

"Jack's Mobile Shop." His opening balance sheet set out in traditional form would have appeared as follows:

BALANCE SHEET OF "JACK'S MOBILE SHOP" AT 1ST JULY

Capital Account—			Motor vehicle	£600
J. Snodgrass	£1,000		Cash in hand	400
	£1,000			£1,000

During July he spent £400 on buying goods all of which he sold for £590. He incurred various business expenses amounting to £65. The results at 31st July would appear thus:

Cash Account

Balance	£400	Purchases A/c	£400
Sales A/c	590	Business Expenses A/c	65
		Balance c/d	525
	£990		£990
Balance b/d	£525		

Trading and Profit and Loss Account

Purchases	£400	Sales	£590
Gross profit	190		
	£590		£590
Business expenses	65	Gross profit	190
Net profit	125		
	£190		£190

It can be seen from the opening balance sheet that when trading commenced the business had £400 in cash available for use. At the end of July the amount of cash available had risen to £525, as shown on the Cash Account. The *increase* in actual cash amounted to £125. The *net profit* on trading for the period also amounted to £125.

We will now show the balance sheet at 31st July but in such a way as to emphasise the relationship between the *abstract* and the *concrete* qualities of the profit which has been made.

BALANCE SHEET AT 31ST JULY

Capital Account—			Motor vehicle	£600
J. Snodgrass	£1,000		Cash in hand at	
			1st July	400
	£1,000			£1,000
Plus:			*Plus:*	
Net profit for period (the			**Net increase in cash** in	
abstract aspect)	125		hand, *i.e.* from	
			£400 to £525 (the	
			concrete aspect)	125
	£1,125			£1,125

Looking at this balance sheet we can clearly see how the two aspects of profit complement one another. The net profit of £125 has been *retained in the business* and has been added to the original capital which Snodgrass invested at the start. He has not removed it from the control of the business even though he was fully entitled to do so had he wished. On the contrary, he has left it with the business thus strengthening its financial position and giving it the opportunity to grow. To put it another way it means, in effect, that Snodgrass has *invested* a further £125 in the business, in addition to the £1,000 which he supplied as his opening capital.

3. Profit is earned on a day-to-day basis. Students of book-keeping are inclined to overlook the fact that *every time* a trader sells some of his stock *a small amount of profit* is made. They tend to look at the *final* amount of profit which is to be seen when the Trading and Profit and Loss Accounts are prepared and think that it is only when these accounts have been produced that any identifiable profit exists. It is true, of course, that the *total* profit for the period *is* suddenly disclosed but many do not appear to comprehend that this final profit figure is the sum-total of *many little bits of profit* earned over *a long period of time*, the accumulated total forming the profit for the period.

PROFIT AND CASH

4. The relationship between profit and cash. So long as *all* transactions are operated on a "cash basis," *i.e.* all payments

and receipts being made by cash and no "non-trading" items
introduced, the net profit will *always* correspond *exactly* to the
increase in cash. This assumes, of course, that goods are sold
for *more* than they cost and that a *profit* is made.

5. The effect of the introduction of "non-trading" items.
When we speak of *"non-trading"* items we mean those payments or receipts which do not have *a direct bearing* on the
actual trading operations, *i.e.* buying and selling. If, for
instance, in the last example Snodgrass had invested *an extra*
£200 in the business the closing balance on the Cash Account
would have been, not £525, but £725, made up as follows:

Opening balance	£400
Add: Extra cash paid in as capital	200
Net profit *on trading*	125
	£725

The *profit* still remains at £125 but the *increase* in the cash
balance from £400 to £725 is made up of an item of £200 from
a *non-trading source* as well as the net profit of £125.

On the other hand let us suppose that far from introducing
additional cash Snodgrass *withdrew* £80 for his own private use.
The Cash Account balance would not be £525 but £445 made
up thus:

Opening balance	£400
Net profit	125
	525
Less: Withdrawn for private use	80
	£445

Once again the *profit* is £125 (as shown in the Profit and Loss
Account) but the cash balance *at the end* has increased by only
£45 from what it was at the start. £80 has been paid out *by* the
business on a *non-trading* matter, *i.e.* on something not connected with *the specific purpose* for which the business was
brought into existence. Thus the financial resources of the
business have been weakened to this extent.

6. The effect of the purchase of fixed assets for cash. The
payment of cash on a non-trading item, but one which ensures

the retention of the money in the business in the form of a
fixed asset, will also cause a divergence from the basic pattern.

Suppose that Snodgrass decided to spend £65 on a particularly accurate set of scales (such as may be seen in many food
shops). Such a payment would *reduce* the cash balance from
£525 to £460. Thus, once again, the *increase* in the opening
cash balance would be *less* than the profit made.

Opening balance	£400
Net profit	125
	525
Less: Purchase of scales	65
	£460

The purchase of the scales is regarded as a non-trading item
even though it is quite directly connected with the business.
The money has not been spent *in the course of* earning profit.
Money spent on petrol or on wages of an assistant *would* be so
regarded. The money spent on the scales was spent *for the
purpose of* earning profit, *e.g.* in making the business more
efficient. The scales at their cost price of £65 may be expected
to appear on all future balance sheets. Thus the *value* of £65 is
retained *within* the business; all that has happened is that it is
no longer a current asset (in the form of cash) but has become a
fixed asset (in the form of scales).

DISPOSING OF PROFIT

7. What happens to the net profit in practice? If all businesses
operated on a "cash" basis and nothing of a non-trading nature
were permitted to take place, the *increase* in the volume of cash
between the beginning and the end of a period of trading would
exactly equal the net profit as shown on the Profit and Loss
Account. *In practice*, of course, this does not happen because
many factors arise making it quite impossible for any business
to carry on without entering into transactions of a non-trading
nature.

The most obvious of these items which comes to mind is
withdrawals of cash by the owner for his private use. It is almost
certain that a small trader will be relying upon the profit

earned *during* a week's trading to give him the means of sub-
sistence for the following week, *i.e.* housekeeping money.

If, on the other hand, his margin of profit is sufficient to
leave part of it in the business week by week, *i.e. after* with-
drawing enough to meet his private needs, this will be reflected
in a *gradual strengthening* of the financial position of the
business. This is called "ploughing back profits" or "retaining
the profits" in the business. Should these "retained" profits
continue to grow, it is natural to expect that the owner will
consider *making use* of them. That is to say, we would expect
to see him try to develop his business by expanding it in some
way with the *additional resources* which the business has now
acquired. There are several ways in which this could be done.

He might, as a beginning, cautiously *expand the amount of
stock carried* and give the customers a wider range of choice. If
this proved successful he might be tempted to *enlarge his
premises* in the expectation that he would increase his sales and
thereby earn even more profit. Again, depending upon the
nature of the business, he might *purchase machines* to manufacture some of the goods he sells instead of buying them
ready-made, or he might consider the *purchase of a delivery van*,
taking customers' orders by telephone, thereby extending the
field of his activities.

8. The effect of non-trading items on profit. The above
suggestions are a few of the ways in which the owner could
make his profits work for him. If he does so it is quite clear that
at the end of the trading period the net profit as shown by the
Profit and Loss Account will have *no recognisable connection*
with the balance on the Cash Account or Bank Account. This,
of course, is due to the intrusion of a variety of items of
expenditure which are largely *non-trading* in nature. However,
even though it may not be possible to *identify* the net profit in
its *concrete* aspect on the assets side we should now be in no
doubt that it does appear there in some form.

9. Credit transactions and the measurement of profit. Up to
this point in our studies we have only dealt with transactions
which have been on a *cash basis*; this term is also intended to
cover transactions which have been settled by means of
cheques. Transactions of a "credit" nature, *i.e.* where payment is made *at a later date*, will be fully dealt with in IX.

For the purposes of the subject-matter of this chapter it is necessary to make reference to transactions of this type. When goods are bought or sold on credit they are treated as purchases or sales in precisely the same way as are cash transactions, and profit is taken where goods are sold in this way *even though the money has not yet been received*. Similarly, goods bought on credit are regarded as purchases and are *debited to the Trading Account* at the end of the period even though they have not been paid for.

In either case the payment is only deferred for a short time, *i.e.* a few weeks usually. Bearing in mind that most accounting periods are of one year's duration "a few weeks" is regarded as a short period of time. As a result of the inclusion of these credit items in the final accounts *the net profit is affected*; that is to say, it will be *increased* by the element of profit contained in those credit *sales* the money for which has not yet been received. To this extent, then, the net profit will basically *not be in agreement* with the increase in the balance on the Cash Account or Bank Account.

The justification for this is that when goods are sold on credit they are sold in the expectation that the money for such sales will be received in due course. Nobody in his senses would sell goods unless he fully expected to be paid for them.

PROGRESS TEST 7

Theory

1. Explain what you understand by the expression "the abstract aspect of profit." (1)
2. What is the other aspect of profit and what form does it take? (2)
3. How and when does profit come about? (3)
4. There is said to be a relationship between profit and cash. Explain this. (4)
5. Give examples of "non-trading" items which may occur during a business year. Will the introduction of such things have any bearing on the relationship between cash and profit? (4, 5)
6. What happens to "net" profit? (7)

Practice

7. Mrs. Jenkins decided to start business as a flower-seller in a street market. She had £30 which she was prepared to invest as the opening capital. Out of this sum she spent £9 on two wicker baskets and £8 on some vases.

Open the ledger accounts and record the above data therein and prepare her opening balance sheet.

She had to pay £3 for the rent of a stall and on each of the next six days she spent £3 on fresh flowers. In addition she paid £1 for a week's supply of tissue paper for wrapping and a total of £2 in fares. By the end of the week she had sold all her flowers for £38.

Enter these transactions in the appropriate ledger accounts. Extract a trial balance and then prepare Trading and Profit and Loss Accounts to ascertain her net profit and a balance sheet to show the final position.

8. Mrs. Jenkins was very pleased with the result of her first week's trading and used £5 of the profit to buy some buckets and some more vases. She took £7 out of the business for her own personal expenses.

During the second week she spent £4 each day on fresh flowers, a further £1 on tissue paper, £2 on fares and £3 for the rent of her stall. By the end of the week she had sold all the flowers for £49.

Enter the second week's transactions in the ledger, extract a trial balance and prepare the final accounts to ascertain her net profit. Finally, draw up a balance sheet to show the final position.

CHAPTER VIII

STOCK

SELLING IS THE KEY TO PROFIT

1. Goods must be sold before any profit is made. This is a statement of the obvious yet one often finds beginners who do not appreciate this simple fact. The reason for it, almost certainly, is that they are struggling to master the rudiments of a new subject and have been taught to place certain items in set positions without properly understanding *why* a particular item should have its place in a particular position.

Let us look at the matter in some detail.

EXAMPLE

A trader buys goods which he expects to resell at a price which is 50 per cent more than he paid for them. He purchased three articles at a cost of £8, £10 and £12 respectively.

	Cost	Sold for	Profit
Item 1	£8	£8 + £4 = £12	£4
,, 2	£10	£10 + £5 = £15	£5
,, 3	£12	£12 + £6 = £18	£6
	£30	£45	£15

We can see clearly that as a result of *selling* his goods he made a gross profit of £15.

The above figures set out in the form of a Trading Account would appear as follows:

Trading Account (I)

Purchase of goods for resale (at *cost* price)	£30	Sales (at *selling* price)	£45
Gross profit	£15		
	£45		£45

Now let us look at the picture supposing that he had not sold
any of the goods. The table would appear thus:

	Cost	Sold for	Profit
Item 1	£8	—	—
,, 2	£10	—	—
,, 3	£12	—	—
	£30	£—	£—

The column headed "Cost" is exactly the same as in the
previous table. The other two columns in the above table have
no entries in them. The conclusion is clear: *No sales mean no
profit.* Set out in Trading Account form:

Trading Account (II)

Purchase of goods for resale (at cost price)	£30	Sales	—

The picture here is incomplete because although the trader
has made no profit he does still possess £30 worth of goods
which he will hope to sell at a later date. These *unsold* goods are
called his "Stock." The *completed* Trading Account would
appear as below:

Trading Account (II) completed

Purchase of goods for resale (at cost price)	£30	Sales Stock of unsold goods (at cost price)	— £30
	£30		£30

The *stock* of unsold goods of £30 which has been credited in the
Trading Account would have to be *debited* to some other account
(in order to *complete* the double entry). In practice we do not
debit this to the "Goods for Resale Account" but to a new
account called "Stock Account."

We will now take the example a stage further, wherein some
of the goods are sold and some are not, in order to emphasise the
point that in order to make a profit goods must be sold.

	Cost	Sold for	Profit	Stock
Item 1	£8	£12	£4	—
,, 2	10	15	5	—
,, 3	12	—	—	£12
	£30	£27	£9	£12

We can see very clearly where the profit has arisen and equally clearly we can see which item of goods has failed to earn any profit.

Trading Account (III)

Purchase of goods for re-sale (at cost price)	£30	Sales (at *selling* price)	£27
Gross profit	9	Stock of unsold goods (at *cost* price)	12
	£39		£39

An alternative method of setting out the Trading Account is:

Trading Account (IV)

Purchase of goods for re-sale	£30	Sales (at *selling* price)	£27
Less Unsold goods (at *cost* price)	12		
Cost price of goods actually sold	£18		
Gross profit	9		
	£27		£27

The layout of Trading Account (IV) is the method which is currently very widely used. The reason for this is that it shows clearly the *cost price of those goods purchased which have actually been sold*. It is by deducting this figure from the sales total that gross profit is ascertained.

2. The defect in the approved method. From the beginner's viewpoint there is a weakness in this last method. The objection to it is that, to some of them at any rate, it is not crystal clear that double-entry is, in fact, being applied. They see *the unsold stock* appearing on the *debit* side of the Trading Account and, as yet, having insufficient expertise in the subject, do not appreciate that a *deduction* from a *debit* item has precisely the same effect as if it had been entered on the *credit* side. If comparison is made between Trading Accounts (III) and (IV), the truth of this statement can be confirmed.

Although this objection may appear to be a trifle pedantic, experience has shown that for some students it is indeed a cause of confusion. To overcome this the writer has devised a method of accounting for stock which, to him, is not only logical but positively desirable.

3. The Purchases Account. Up to this point all goods purchased with a view to their being sold have been entered in a "Goods for Resale Account." This heading has been used for the express purpose of clarity; in order to show the student the *intention* behind the purchase of the goods, *i.e.* that they have been bought with the sole object of being resold at a *higher* figure which, when it does take place, will bring some profit to the business.

In future, we will use the account heading for these goods which is in general use, namely, the "Purchases Account."

4. Using the Purchases Account to deal with stock. When goods are bought for resale the cost will be debited to the Purchases Account. In all but the most exceptional circumstances *some* of these goods will *not* have been sold at the end of a period of trading. This is to be expected. However, the owner knows that they will be sold during the next trading period and therefore they must be *carried forward* into that new period. For the purposes of the final accounts and the balance sheet these *surplus* goods will be referred to as "the *closing* stock." That is to say that in the balance sheet the closing stock will be treated as an *asset* which, of course, is perfectly logical. If this stock had not been purchased there would have been more money left in the Bank Account and we most certainly treat "Cash at Bank" as an asset. The closing stock thus represents *money* which is temporarily tied up in the asset of "Stock."

As was shown in the example in **1**, this unsold stock has a part to play when the gross profit is being calculated. Stock which has *not* been sold *must be eliminated* because it has not played any part in the earning of the profit. The important calculation is to ascertain the cost of those goods *which have actually been sold*.

The method which is about to be suggested first brings the "closing" stock into the Purchases Account *on the credit side* whence it is *carried down* as a *debit* balance. It thus becomes the "Opening Stock" of the new period, in exactly the same way as the balance on the Bank Account, having been brought down, is the *opening* figure of "Cash at Bank" for the new period.

We are now left with a gap on the credit side of the Purchases Account. This represents the "Cost of Goods Sold" which is the *essential* figure required for the Trading Account. If desired the transfer may be made direct to the Trading Account but it is felt that it might be better to make the transfer to a fresh account called "Cost of Goods Sold Account." The final transfer would be made from here to the Trading Account.

EXAMPLE

The purchases of goods made by a business during its first year of trading amounted to £4,250. At the end of the year the unsold stock *at cost* totalled £680. The sales for the year were £4,920.

Stage 1. First of all let us open the Sales and Purchases Accounts and record the respective totals.

Bank Account

Sales A/c	£4,920	Purchases A/c	£4,250

Purchases Account

Bank A/c	£4,250	

Sales Account

	Bank A/c	£4,920

Stage 2. Here we will introduce the *closing* stock.

Purchases Account

Bank A/c (per Stage 1)	£4,250	Unsold stock c/d	£680
Unsold stock b/d	£680		

Stage 3. As can be seen there is a big gap between the amounts on the debit and credit sides of the Purchases Account. This must now be *filled in* and the double entry completed by debiting the "Cost of Goods Sold Account" with the difference.

Purchases Account

Bank A/c (per Stage 1)	£4,250	**Cost of Goods Sold A/c**	**£3,570**
		Unsold stock c/d	680
	£4,250		£4,250
Unsold stock b/d	£680		

Cost of Goods Sold Account

Purchases A/c	£3,570		

Stage 4. We can now complete the entries and ascertain the gross profit.

Cost of Goods Sold Account

Purchases A/c (per Stage 3)	£3,570	**Trading A/c**	**£3,570**

Trading Account

Cost of Goods Sold A/c	£3,570	Sales A/c (per Stage 1)	£4,920
Gross profit (to Profit & Loss A/c)	1,350		
	£4,920		£4,920

Profit and Loss Account

	Gross profit (from Trading A/c) £1,350

If the *traditional* method were used the Trading Account would have appeared as follows:

Trading Account

Purchases A/c	£4,250	Sales A/c	£4,920
Gross profit (to Profit & Loss A/c)	1,350	**Stock A/c** (unsold goods)	**680**
	£5,600		£5,600

Stock Account

Trading A/c	£680	

TRADITIONAL METHOD OF DEALING WITH STOCK

5. The traditional method and the trial balance. When the traditional method is used the Stock Account carries the debit balance (representing the value of *unsold* goods) into the *new period*. *During* this subsequent period of trading *no further entry is made in this Stock Account*.

All *new purchases* of goods will be debited in the Purchases Account and so the ledger will carry *two* accounts concerned with *goods for resale*. When the time comes for the preparation of the trial balance the balances on both the Stock Account *and* the Purchases Account will have to appear *separately* on it.

6. The traditional method and the entries at the end of the year. When this subsequent trading period comes to an end and the trial balance has been agreed the appropriate ledger accounts will be closed off and the Trading Account prepared. In dealing with the entries in the *Trading Account* the first matter will be to debit it with the balance of *opening stock* from the Stock Account, thus *temporarily* closing off this account.

Next, the Purchases Account will be closed by a transfer to the Trading Account and the Sales Account likewise.

The *closing* stock at the end of this second period will now be valued and entered on the *credit* side of the Trading Account. (Alternatively, it may be set on the *debit side* and *deducted* from the total of both Opening Stock and Purchases.) Whichever form is used in the Trading Account a fresh *debit* entry must now be made in the Stock Account.

EXAMPLE

Continuing the previous example, the opening stock for the second period of trading stands at £680. During the year purchases of goods totalled £5,410 and sales were £6,925. Closing stock *at cost* was valued at £942.

Stage 1. The entries in the Purchases, Sales and Bank Accounts would be:

Bank Account

Sales A/c	£6,925	Purchases A/c	£5,410

Purchases Account

Bank A/c	£5,410

Sales Account

	Bank A/c	£6,925

It must be remembered that we will need to bring *the opening balance* of the Stock Account into consideration since undoubtedly part of the sales will have been made from some or all of the items contained in the opening stock. Hence:

Stock Account

Balance b/f	£680

Stage 2. Let us now close off both the Stock and the Purchases Accounts.

Stock Account

| Balance b/f | £680 | **Trading A/c** | £680 |

Purchases Account

| Bank A/c (per Stage 1) | £5,410 | **Trading A/c** | £5,410 |

Trading Account

Stock A/c (Opening balance)	£680		
Purchases A/c	5,410		
	£6,090		

The balance on the Trading Account, £6,090 represents the *total cost* of all goods which have been *available* for sale *during* the year.

Stage 3. We will now transfer, or *post* (to use the usual term) the balance from the Sales Account to the Trading Account and leave the stage clear to deal with the *closing* stock.

Sales Account

| **Trading A/c** | £6,925 | Bank A/c (per Stage 1) | £6,925 |

Trading Account

| Balance (per Stage 2) | £6,090 | **Sales A/c** | £6,925 |

Stage 4. No matter which of the two alternative methods available we use, the Stock Account *must be debited* with the value of the *closing* stock.

Dealing with the *old* straightforward double-entry method we obtain the following result:

Trading Account

Balance (per Stage 3)	£6,090	Sales A/c (per Stage 3)	£6,925
		Stock A/c (unsold goods)	942
			£7,867

Up to this point, the Stock Account had nothing in it since it had been closed off in Stage 2 and no balance was left on it at that point.

Stock Account

Trading A/c £942	

The balance of £942 will now be carried forward into the third trading period as the *opening* stock of that period.

Stage 5. The Trading Account can now be completed and the gross profit ascertained.

Trading Account

Opening stock	£680	Sales (per Stage 4)	£6,925
Purchases	5,410	Closing stock (per Stage 4)	942
	6,090		
Gross profit	1,777		
	£7,867		£7,867

If we use the currently accepted method of presentation, the Trading Account would be set out in the following manner:

Trading Account

Opening stock	£680	Sales	£6,925
Purchases	5,410		
	6,090		
Less Closing stock	942		
Cost of goods sold	5,148		
Gross profit	1,777		
	£6,925		£6,925

The principal virtue of this method is that it does give us the *cost of goods sold*. It is contended, however, that for the beginner, at least, there is the danger that the *debit/credit* aspect of the closing stock entries may not be readily discernible. Furthermore, it *does not* eliminate the beginner's confusion over the transfer of the opening as well as closing stocks to the Trading Account. This latter point is a very real danger.

AN EFFECTIVE ALTERNATIVE METHOD

7. The benefit of combining the stock and purchases in one account. We will now place the figures of this last example in an account *combining stock* and *purchases made* during the year. The opening stock of £680 will be used as the starting point.

Purchases Account

Balance (at start of period) b/d	£680	Cost of Goods Sold A/c	£5,148
Bank A/c (purchases made during the year)	5,410	Stock c/d	942
	£6,090		£6,090
Balance b/d	£942		

Cost of Goods Sold Account

Purchases A/c	**£5,148**	Trading A/c	£5,148

Trading Account

Cost of Goods Sold A/c	£5,148	Sales	£6,925
Gross profit	1,777		
	£6,925		£6,925

The *simplicity* of this method is clearly seen from the above accounts.

8. Closing stock and the trial balance. Where the *traditional* method is employed, whether it be the older or the newer version, the "opening stock" must *always* be entered as a *separate* item in the trial balance. This, of course, is clearly necessary because it was one of the *opening* balances at the *start* of the period in exactly the same way as, say, the balance on Shop Fittings Account might be. No *subsequent* entries will have been made on the debit side of the Stock Account.

The "closing stock" will *never* appear in the trial balance under either form of the *traditional* method. The reason for this, of course, is that the stock which remains unsold *at the end of the period* is a part of:

(*a*) the opening stock (possibly), and
(*b*) goods purchased *during* the period.

As both of these items are *already* debited in the trial balance the *closing* stock is *automatically* included therein.

If the method of *combining* both stock and purchases in the same account is employed, we ascertain in one operation the cost price of those goods which have actually been sold, *i.e.* we *deduct* the closing stock from the total of, both the opening stock and the purchases made during the period. It follows, therefore, that if we enter *only* the "Cost of Goods Sold" in the trial balance, the debit side will be short. It thus becomes necessary to enter the *closing* stock as well *in order to balance*. One of the important benefits of this method of treatment is that the trial balance will then contain *every* figure required for the preparation of both the Trading and Profit and Loss Accounts. The only item which does not appear and which will be required for the construction of the balance sheet is the "net profit." This will emerge on the completion of the Profit and Loss Account.

EXAMPLE

Suppose the opening stock amounted to £1,750 and that goods to the value of £10,200 were purchased during the period. At the end of the year closing stock was found to be £1,600.

Traditional method		*Suggested method*	
Opening stock	£1,750	Opening stock	£1,750
Purchases	10,200	Purchases	10,200
			11,950
		Less Closing stock	1,600
	£11,950	Cost of goods sold	£10,350
Entries in trial balance		*Entries in trial balance*	
Opening stock	£1,750	Cost of goods sold	£10,350
Purchases	10,200	*Closing* stock	1,600
Total	£11,950	Total	£11,950

As can be seen the *total* amount to be debited in the trial balance is £11,950 *whichever method is used*, and, as a result, the trial balance will remain in balance. The important point to be appreciated about the "Suggested Method" is that the "Cost of Goods Sold" is ready and waiting to be placed in the Trading Account for the immediate calculation of the "Gross Profit" and, in addition, the "Closing Stock" can be taken straight into the Balance Sheet.

The next example will take the reader through a complete trading period and enable him to evaluate the benefit of operating a Cost of Goods Sold Account as well as incorporating the closing stock in the trial balance.

EXAMPLE

The balance sheet of "Robertson's Stores" at the end of the first year of trading on 31st December 19-0 was as follows:

BALANCE SHEET

Liabilities		*Assets*	
Capital—		Shop fittings	£695
A. Robertson	£5,780	Motor van	420
		Stock of goods	3,657
		Cash at bank	1,008
	£5,780		£5,780

During the second year of trading all transactions were settled through the Bank Account. These were as follows:

Purchases of goods	£12,320
Sales	16,857
Rent	500
Rates	142
Light and heat	95
Drawings	2,400

Stock at the end of the year, valued at cost, amounted to £3,820.

Stage **1.** It is *vitally* important that as a first step ledger accounts be opened for each item appearing in the balance sheet. If this is done we will have a ledger which is *in balance* at the start. The immense importance of this is that when we take *each* of the transactions individually (which have taken place at a later date) and apply the technique of *double* entry, our ledger will continue to *remain* in balance. We should thus have no difficulty in agreeing our trial balance at the end of the year.

Capital Account—A. Robertson

	19–0
	Dec. 31 Balance b/d £5,780

Shop Fittings Account

19–0	
Dec. 31 Balance b/d £695	

Motor Van Account

19–0	
Dec. 31 Balance b/d £420	

Stock of Goods Account or *Purchases Account*

19–0	
Dec. 31 Balance b/d (opening stock) £3,657	

Bank Account

19–0	
Dec. 31 Balance b/d £1,008	

Having opened up the respective ledger accounts it is always advisable to add up the balances on both sides to make sure that they agree and thus ensure that no mistake has been made when transferring the figures.

It will be observed that the balance of *opening* stock has been entered temporarily under a dual heading, to avoid confusion at this point. In the stages which follow the heading "Purchases Account" will be used.

Stage 2. In this section we will deal with the transactions relating to purchases and sales only.

Bank Account

Balance (per Stage 1)	£1,008	Purchases A/c	£12,320
Sales A/c	16,857	Balance c/d	5,545
	£17,865		£17,865
Balance b/d	£5,545		

Purchases Account

Balance of stock (per Stage 1) b/d	£3,657
Bank A/c	12,320
	£15,977

Sales Account

	Bank A/c	£16,857

Stage 3. Next, we will calculate the cost of goods sold.

Purchases Account

Balance (per Stage 1)	£3,657	———————	*
Bank A/c	12,320	Balance c/d (Unsold stock at end of year)	£3,820
	£15,977		
Balance b/d	£3,820		

At this moment we have to insert a missing figure on the credit side on the line marked *. This missing figure will, of course, be *the cost price of those goods which have been sold*.

Subtracting £3,820 from £15,977 we obtain a sum of £12,157 which, of course, is *the cost of goods sold*. This amount would therefore be *credited* to Purchases Account and *debited* as below.

Cost of Goods Sold Account

Purchases A/c	£12,157	

Stage 4. Our next task is to make the entries relating to the expenses.

Bank Account

Balance (per Stage 2)	£5,545	Rent A/c	£500
		Rates A/c	142
		Light and Heat A/c	95
			737
		Balance c/d	4,808
	£5,545		£5,545
Balance b/d	£4,808		

Rent Account

| Bank A/c | £500 | |

Rates Account

| Bank A/c | £142 | |

Light and Heat Account

| Bank A/c | £95 | |

Stage 5. Robertson's drawings of £2,400 cash will now be recorded.

Bank Account

Balance (per Stage 4)	£4,808	Capital A/c—Drawings	£2,400
		Balance c/d	2,408
	£4,808		£4,808
Balance b/d	£2,408		

Capital Account—A. Robertson

Bank A/c—Drawings	£2,400	Balance (per Stage 1)	£5,780
Balance c/d	3,380		
	£5,780		£5,780
		Balance b/d	£3,380

Stage 6. At this point we will check our entries by means of a Trial Balance.

TRIAL BALANCE

	Debit	Credit
Shop Fittings A/c (Stage 1)	£695	
Motor Vans A/c (Stage 1)	420	
Sales A/c (Stage 2)		£16,857
Closing Stock per Purchases A/c (Stage 3)	3,820	
Cost of Goods Sold A/c (Stage 3)	12,157	
Rent A/c (Stage 4)	500	
Rates A/c (Stage 4)	142	
Light and Heat A/c (Stage 4)	95	
Bank A/c (Stage 5)	2,408	
Capital A/c (Stage 5)		3,380
	£20,237	£20,237

Stage 7. We must now summarise those accounts which have a bearing on the final accounts and we will complete the necessary postings.

Sales Account

Trading A/c	£16,857	Balance (per Stage 2)	£16,857

Cost of Goods Sold Account

Balance (per Stage 3)	£12,157	**Trading A/c**	£12,157

Rent Account

Balance (per Stage 4)	£500	**Profit and Loss A/c**	£500

Rates Account

| Balance (per Stage 4) | £142 | **Profit and Loss A/c** | £142 |

Light and Heat Account

| Balance (per Stage 4) | £95 | **Profit and Loss A/c** | £95 |

(The transfers to the Trading Account and to the Profit and Loss Account are shown in **heavy type** in order to give emphasis to the closing entries.)

NOTE: Special attention is drawn to the presentation of the "final" accounts. These *two* accounts are invariably shown under the heading "Trading and Profit and Loss Account," *i.e.* as though they form *one* account only but comprising *two separate sections*. Note also that the use of the abbreviation "A/c" is *not* normally entered in either of the "final" accounts in respect of the various items entered therein.

Trading and Profit and Loss Account

Cost of Goods Sold	£12,157	Sales	£16,857
Gross profit c/d	4,700		
	£16,857		£16,857
Rent	£500	Gross Profit b/d	£4,700
Rates	142		
Light and heat	95		
	£737		
Net profit transferred to Capital Account	3,963		
	£4,700		£4,700

Stage 9. Here we come to the *very last entry*, the posting of the *net* profit to Robertson's Capital Account.

Capital Account—A. Robertson

Balance c/d	£7,343	Balance (per Stage 5)	£3,380
		Profit and Loss	
		Account net profit	3,963
	£7,343		£7,343
		Balance b/d	£7,343

Stage 10. The final stage has now been reached and the balance sheet is set out below in traditional form.

BALANCE SHEET AS AT 31ST DECEMBER, 19–1

Liabilities				*Assets*	
Capital Account				Shop Fittings Account (Stage 1)	£695
Balance at 1st January 19–1	£5,780			Motor Van Account (Stage 1)	420
Add Net profit for year	3,963			Stock, *i.e.* Purchases Account (Stage 3)	3,820
	9,743			Bank Account (Stage 7)	2,408
Less Drawings	2,400				
		£7,343			
		£7,343			£7,343

THE VALUATION OF STOCK

9. Taking stock. For a business to know the amount of gross profit it has made during a period of trading it has to calculate the cost of goods sold, *i.e.* how much those goods which have been sold cost at the time of purchase, and *deduct* this figure from the value of the sales. The *difference* between these two amounts is the gross profit.

The cost of goods sold is obtained by adding the value (at *cost* price) of the stock in hand *at the start of the period* to the value of the goods purchased *during* the period and, from the total so obtained, *deducting* the value (at *cost* price again) of the stock *at the end* of the period.

In exercises and in examination problems the figure of "closing stock" is always given. In real life, however, it has to be ascertained by means of what is known as the "annual stock-taking" which should be done immediately the end of the financial year is reached. If it is not done then complications arise owing to the fact that *on and after* the first day of the new period goods will be *sold*. The sales made on even one day may be quite difficult to evaluate at cost price since no detailed check would be kept on the items actually sold. Consider for a moment a large store or a grocery supermarket which may very well sell thousands of different items; then imagine the complex task involved in ascertaining how many of which type were sold and the *cost price* of each one. This would be necessary because at the end of the *previous* trading period, *i.e.* the night before, every one of those items formed part of the *closing* stock. It can be seen, therefore, that taking stock is a vital part of the life of a business, and how necessary it is that the *physical* goods actually in stock are *counted* and recorded in "stock sheets." The value of these items can be calculated later on.

Additional, but less difficult, problems are caused by *deliveries* of fresh goods immediately after the year end which are placed *in stock*. These must obviously be *excluded* from the count if the stocktaking is delayed. Their value can, of course, be easily ascertained from the invoices relating to them.

10. The entries in the stock sheets. When stock is being "taken" it is of extreme importance that a number of things be done and done *correctly*. If the various tasks are not carried out with care the gross profit will be affected. Too *high* a valuation placed on "closing" stock will *increase* the figure of gross profit shown on the Trading Account. Conversely, too low a value will decrease that figure.

EXAMPLE

The opening stock of a business was £5,720. Purchases during the year amounted to £66,475 and sales were £94,640. Let us take three *different* figures for the *closing* stock, the *correct one* being £6,150.

	Opening stock	Purchases	Closing stock (deduct)	Cost of sales
Low	£5,720	£66,475	£5,850 =	£66,345
Correct	£5,720	£66,475	£6,150 =	£66,045
High	£5,720	£66,475	£6,500 =	£65,695

The gross profits would be:

	Low	Correct	High
Sales	£94,640	£94,640	£94,640
Cost of sales (as above)	£66,345	£66,045	£65,695
Gross profit	£28,295	£28,595	£28,945

The example shows clearly how the gross profit can be affected by an incorrect "stock take." The important matters to be watched at stocktaking are as follows:

(a) Each item must be counted *physically* and the *total* entered in a column headed "Quantity."

(b) In the next column the *cost price* of the type of article must be shown. This will normally be obtainable from the invoices. There may be difficulty in deciding upon this if the cost has varied recently, but we are concerned here only with the general principle and so we will not discuss that aspect in this book.

(c) The third column should show the value in *money*. This is obtainable by multiplying the quantity by the price.

(d) The *additions* of the third column must be made correctly in order to ascertain the *total value* of the closing stock.

If the amount of stock carried is large some careful organisation will be required for the carrying out of the stocktaking. Great care will need to be exercised, in many cases, to ensure that items are neither omitted nor counted twice, for, as we have shown, the gross profit will be wrong if any of the four tasks outlined above are not correctly performed.

11. The basis of stock valuation. In the preceding section we have spoken of closing stock being valued at cost. This is, indeed, the normal valuation placed on it but circumstances can arise which would make this basis of valuation wrong. Where, as does sometimes happen, the unsold goods (or a portion of them) deteriorate or become obsolete, the possibility of selling them at the ordinary selling price is, as a result, very unlikely. It becomes necessary therefore to use a different basis upon which to value these goods; that valuation is known as "current market value." The meaning applied to that term is that the goods should be valued at whatever figure, *no* *matter how small,* the owner of the business thinks he may obtain. Very often in practice this means almost giving them away.

Students are urged to memorise the following expression:

*Closing stock must be valued at either cost or current market value, **whichever is the lower.***

ACCOUNTING RATIOS CONNECTED WITH STOCK

12. The percentage of gross profit. A very important ratio used by accountants is that whereby the gross profit is expressed as a *percentage* of the total sales. Thus, if the sales amounted to £40,000 and the gross profit were £10,000 we would say that "the gross profit amounted to 25% of sales." To obtain the percentage we use the formula:

$$\frac{\text{Gross Profit} \times 100}{\text{Sales}}$$

Using the figures given in the preceding paragraph we would show:

$$\frac{£10,000 \times 100}{£40,000} = 25\%$$

An easy way to remember the formula is to add *two noughts* to the gross profit and then divide by the sales. It is suggested that students who have not met the formula before should accustom themselves to making the calculation by practising with a variety of figures for the gross profit and the sales. Examiners often ask for the percentage of gross profit as part of the answer to a problem and a very useful mark or two may be earned as a result.

13. The meaning of the gross profit percentage. One finds many students capable of calculating the gross profit percentage but who do not understand precisely what it means or for what reason it is employed.

The meaning underlying it is that whatever percentage is revealed is the *number of pounds* (sterling) of gross profit earned by *each* £100 of *sales* made by the business. Thus, for example, a gross profit percentage of 35 per cent means that for every £100 of sales made £35 has been earned as gross profit.

14. The use of the percentage of gross profit. This percentage gives the owner (and also the Inspector of Taxes) a very useful guide to the profitability of the business. Normally, the percentage should not vary very much from year to year. Comparisons between years can be very helpful in directing the management of a business, for it must be remembered that the gross profit is the life-blood of every business. Out of it must come all the running expenses which are charged in the Profit and Loss Account and there must remain a reasonable figure of net profit to reward the owner.

If the gross profit percentage figure shows a marked difference with that of earlier years the owner will be alerted to the fact that something may be amiss. If, for example, some goods had not been brought into the calculation of closing stock the gross profit would be less than it should be. Figures alone will, very possibly, not show clearly that something is wrong. This is particularly so where figures are large bearing in mind that they are not normally in round hundreds or thousands. By applying the formula we can see at a glance that something may appear to be radically wrong. If, for instance, the *normal* gross profit percentage was 35 per cent but suddenly dropped to, say, 28 per cent one would immediately sense that something was wrong and all of the figures in the Trading Account would be suspect. Enquiries would begin at once and every effort would be made to track down the source of the error, if, in fact, a mistake had been made. For instance, *invoices* for goods could have been received just before the end of the year, the Purchases Account being debited and the suppliers' accounts credited. The *goods* themselves may have been delayed in transit and, therefore, *not taken into stock*. Thus the cost of sales would be greater than it should be, giving a lower figure of gross profit than would otherwise have been the case. As a result, the gross profit percentage would also be lower than it should be. Again, sales may have been made and the necessary entries put through the books, but the goods may not have been despatched to the customer and by mistake are *included* in the closing stock. In such a case the gross profit itself would appear as more than it should be, since the Sales Account had been credited while the closing stock was inflated by the cost of those goods which had not been sent to the customer.

15. The rate of stock turnover. When we speak of the "turnover of stock" we mean the *sale* of those goods specifically bought for the purpose of being sold. Thus a trader might spend £2,000 on his original stock of goods. When these have all been sold we say that he has "turned his stock over." By selling, or turning over his stock he makes a certain amount of profit. It follows that the *more often* he turns his stock over the *greater* will be the profit.

EXAMPLE

A, B and C all open similar businesses on the same day, each one investing £2,000 in the purchase of goods for resale. The gross profit made for each business was at the rate of $33\frac{1}{3}$ per cent of the selling price. A turns his stock over once in the year, B twice and C four times.

The amounts of gross profit will therefore be:

Number of times stock is turned over during year		Sales for year	Gross profit	
A	1	£3,000	£1,000	($33\frac{1}{3}$% of £3,000)
B	2	£6,000	£2,000	(,, ,, £6,000)
C	4	£12,000	£4,000	(,, ,, £12,000)

From this example it is plain to see that the speed of turnover, *i.e.* the number of times the stock is sold out, replaced and then sold again, is a matter of great importance to a trader.

16. Calculating the rate of stock turnover. To ascertain the rate at which a trader turns his stock over the following simple formula is used:

$$\frac{\text{Cost of goods sold}}{\text{Average stock held}} = \text{Rate of stock turnover}$$

i.e. the number of times a trader's stock is sold out during a period of trading.

17. The average amount of stock held. For examination purposes we are, as a general rule, only given the amounts of the *opening* and the *closing* stocks. These two amounts are then added together and divided by two and the result is, of course, the *average*. This presupposes that similar amounts of stock are held on the average throughout the year and it is probably reasonably true of the great majority of businesses. In practice one does not normally find wide differences between opening and closing stocks, although, of course, it does sometimes occur.

EXAMPLE

A trader's opening stock was £2,400 and his closing stock £2,600. The *cost* of goods sold during the year was £15,000. The average stock was:

$$\frac{£2,400 + £2,600}{2} = £2,500$$

So: $\dfrac{£15,000 \text{ (cost of goods sold)}}{£2,500 \text{ (average stock)}} = 6$ (rate of stock turnover)

We thus conclude that he turned his stock over six times during the year. Since he turned his stock over every *two months*, *i.e.* six times in the year, it is fair to say that with each separate turnover of stock he earned one-sixth of the year's gross profit.

PROGRESS TEST 8

Theory

1. In order to make a trading profit what is the one essential requirement? **(1, 4)**

2. Describe in detail how you would try to convince a beginner that the amount spent on the purchase of goods for resale was not the criterion by which profit is calculated. **(1)**

3. Describe the traditional way of dealing with closing stock at the end of a period of trading. What important piece of information is lacking if this method is used? **(5, 6)**

4. How can we obtain the cost of goods sold by means of an effective alternative method? **(4, 7)**

5. By what means is the value of the closing stock calculated? **(9)**

6. Set out in detail the matters you would pay particular attention to when "taking stock." **(10)**

7. On what basis must closing stock be valued? **(11)**

8. What do you understand by the expression "the percentage of gross profit"? How is it ascertained? **(12, 13)**

9. Set out the information which the gross profit percentage may give to the owner of a business. **(14)**

10. What is meant by the "rate of stock turnover"? How is it calculated? **(15, 16, 17)**

Practice

11. William Wilcox paid £450 out of his private funds into a business bank account. The following transactions were then entered into (all items being passed through the Bank Account):

Nov. 2	Purchased goods for resale at a cost of	£194
3	Paid for shop equipment	180
4	Sold goods for cash	59
7	Paid wages	12
9	Purchased papers bags for wrapping goods	6
11	Further cash sales to date	57
14	Purchased goods for resale	48
19	Paid wages	24
23	Drew cash for own personal use	20
30	Cash sales	65

Closing stock on 30th November was valued at cost at £143.

Enter the above transactions in the ledger of the business and extract a trial balance as at 30th November. When this has been agreed prepare a Trading Account, a Profit and Loss Account and a balance sheet.

12. T. Hawkins commenced business on 1st July with £750 in the bank and a stock of goods which had cost him £1,630. During July the following transactions took place:

July 1	Paid one month's rent for shop	£50
3	Cash sales	82
8	Drew cash from bank for own use	40
12	Cash sales	174
15	Purchased goods	45
18	Paid for repairs to shop window	17
20	Cash sales	209
24	Bought office safe	85
27	Purchased goods	66
31	Cash sales	284

Closing stock at 31st July was valued at cost, £1,246.

All cash sales were paid into the bank on the dates shown above and all payments were by cheque. Enter all the matters set out above in the ledger accounts and extract a trial balance. Close off the accounts and prepare a Trading and Profit and Loss Account for the month and show a balance sheet as at 31st July.

Show also the percentage of gross profit to the sales and indicate the cost of sales.

13. T. Hawkins continued his business during the month of August. He opened a Cash Account in addition to the Business Bank Account. The transactions during the month of August

were as follows, all cash sales being banked on the dates mentioned below:

Aug.1	Drew cheque for £25 in cash which was used to open the Cash Account	
2	Paid one month's rent by cheque	£50
3	Bought postage stamps for cash	4
5	Purchased goods paying by cheque	86
7	Cash sales to date	301
10	Paid travelling expenses in cash	5
11	Paid Chamber of Commerce subscription by cheque	10
12	Purchased goods for cash	14
14	Cash sales for the week	287
15	Drew cheque for cash (for the Cash Account)	25
17	Drew cheque for cash for his own use	50
19	Purchased goods paying by cheque	226
21	Cash sales for the week	410
24	Purchased cleaning materials for cash	3
28	Cash sales for the week	367
31	Paid assistant's wages in cash	20

Closing stock at 31st August, valued at cost, amounted to £666. Enter all the above transactions in the ledger and then extract a trial balance. Prepare a Trading and Profit and Loss account for August and show the balance sheet as at 31st August. Indicate the cost of sales and calculate the percentage of gross profit to sales.

14. A business held in stock 6,000 articles of the same type at the start of its trading year. These were valued at £2 each. During the year 42,000 similar articles were bought at an average cost of £2·25. All sales were at £3 per article. At the end of the year the stock amounted to 5,000 articles. What amount of gross profit was made during the year? (You are to assume that the opening stock was all sold during the year.)

15. M. Ellery's opening stock amounted to £1,250. During the year he made purchases of £14,200 and his sales totalled £20,780. He worked on a gross profit margin of 30% on his sales. Calculate the cost of goods sold and ascertain the value of his closing stock. What was the rate of stock turnover (calculated to the nearest decimal point)?

16. M. Ellery continued to trade for a further year starting with the closing stock as ascertained from the previous question. Sales amounted to £25,690 and his closing stock was £1,402. He continued to work on a gross profit margin of 30%.

Show his Trading Account for the year:

(a) by the traditional method;

    (b) by showing the closing stock as a deduction from opening stock and purchases total; and

    (c) by the "cost of goods sold" method.

Calculate the rate of stock turnover during the period.

17. S. Laxton dealt in one standard type of product. For several years past the buying price had remained unchanged and at the beginning of his present trading year his stock consisted of 1,300 units which had cost £10 each. During the year he made the following purchases:

29th January	1,000 units at £10 each	All sold
30th May	1,200 units at £9 each	All sold
31st July	900 units at £7 each	All sold
17th September	500 units at £6 each	300 sold
23rd November	800 units at £9 each	None sold
31st December	600 units at £8 each	None sold

Sales during the year amounted to 4,700 units at £15 each.

Assuming that the cost has now been stabilised at £8 per unit, prepare a Trading Account showing in detail your calculation of the value of the closing stock. State your reasons for valuing the stock in the way you have.

CHAPTER IX

CREDIT TRANSACTIONS

CASH AND CREDIT TRANSACTIONS COMPARED

1. Cash transactions. Up to this point in our studies the buying and selling of all goods has been carried out by means of "ready-money" transactions. That is to say, payment was made *at the same time* as the goods passed from the possession of the seller to the buyer. This is the normal practice when one goes into a shop to buy, for example, a packet of cigarettes. The shopkeeper would record it as a sale for *cash*. The buyer would call it, from his viewpoint, a *cash* purchase.

2. The problem facing the seller. Consider the position of the shopkeeper who sells the cigarettes. As he expects to sell a good many packets of cigarettes to his customers every day he needs to maintain a comparatively large stock. This means that he must be prepared to invest what, for him, may amount to a lot of money. Let us suppose that his shop is in a position to do a fairly big trade but that he has not enough money to stock it to its full potential. What is he to do? The usual course is for him to approach the manufacturers or wholesalers and ask them to sell the cigarettes to him **on credit**.

Looking back to Chapter II we recall that a person who entrusts something of value to another person without payment, is called a "creditor." Hence, a transaction involving the transference of goods from the possession of the seller to that of the buyer *without any money passing* in settlement is called a "credit" transaction.

3. Sales of goods on credit. It is necessary to point out here that when goods are sold a legal contract is entered into. The *essence* of such a contract is that the seller agrees to part with his property on the understanding that the buyer will pay the price agreed between them—either *now or later*.

Let us now see how we may apply the rules of double-entry

book-keeping to transactions which involve the use of the *credit* medium. First of all we will look at a sale of goods for *cash* and then we will examine a sale *on credit* so that we may compare them.

EXAMPLE

Goods are sold on 5th July for £80, settlement being made *immediately* by cheque.

Bank Account

July 5 Sales A/c	£80	

Sales Account

	July 5 Bank A/c	£80

EXAMPLE

On 5th July, goods are sold *on credit* to a customer, F. Hill, for £125. The following entries must be made:

F. Hill Account

July 9 Sales A/c	£125	

Sales Account

	July 9 F. Hill A/c	£125

If we now compare the two examples it is clear that they have one thing in common: *in each case* the Sales Account is *credited*.

The essential difference between the two transactions is that in the first case the *money* has been *received* (and paid into the bank), while in the second case we have received no money but possess a legal claim on *a debtor* instead, *i.e.* someone who *owes money to us*.

EXAMPLE

To complete matters Hill pays £125 on 11th August.

F. Hill Account

July 5	Sales A/c	£125	Aug. 11	**Bank A/c**	**£125**

Bank Account

Aug. 11	**F. Hill A/c**	£125

Sales Account

	July 9	F. Hill A/c £125

Looking back to the first two examples we can see that the operations are, *ultimately*, identical; the only difference being the *date* upon which the *cash was received*.

Hill's account has been closed off because he no longer *owes* us anything. During the period of *waiting* (for payment) he showed up very clearly as a *debtor* (*see* the second example above) and at that stage his personal account was of great importance. Now that *he has paid his debt* his account has no particular significance other than that of historical interest, indicating that he has had business dealings with us during the period.

4. Purchasing goods on credit. Exactly the same technique is used where goods are bought on credit as that employed for selling goods on credit. The following example should make this clear.

EXAMPLE

Goods for resale are purchased for £60 on 9th July and are paid for by cheque *at the time of purchase*. We will assume that there was a balance of £100 in the Bank Account.

Bank Account

July 9	Balance b/d	£100	July 9	Purchase of Goods A/c	£60

Purchase of Goods Account

July 9	Bank A/c	£60

EXAMPLE

Goods for resale are bought *on credit* on 14th July from A. Dale costing £94.

A. Dale Account

	July 14	Purchase of Goods A/c	£94

Purchase of Goods Account

July 14	A. Dale A/c	£94	

Examining the first example in **4**, all that has happened is that we have made a simple *exchange* of cash for goods. That is to say we have *received* some goods (but now have *less* money than we had before).

The situation in the second example in **4** is a little different. In this case the total sum of our assets has *increased* by £94 due to the *addition to our stock* of goods of that amount. At the same time we find that our *liabilities have increased by a similar amount, i.e.* by the £94 which is *owed by us* to Dale.

EXAMPLE

In order to close the matter we will suppose that we pay Dale £94 on August 23rd.

A. Dale Account

Aug. 23	Bank A/c	£94	July 14	Purchase of Goods A/c	£94

Bank Account

	Aug. 23	A. Dale A/c	£94

Purchase of Goods Account

July 14	A. Dale A/c	£94	

With the completion of the entries the essential *similarity* of the two transactions can be seen quite clearly and can be summarised as follows:

	Goods purchased		*Cash paid*	
July 9th	£60	July 9th	£60
July 14th	94	Aug. 23rd	94
	£154		£154

In the preceding examples in this chapter, the key point to watch is the dates.

RETURNING GOODS TO THE SUPPLIER

5. Purchase returns. Occasionally, goods which have been purchased *on credit* have to be sent back to the supplier for some reason, *e.g.* they may be of faulty construction. Since these goods have been treated as a *purchase* in the books, *i.e.* they have been debited to the Purchase of Goods Account, it will now be necessary to make a *correcting entry* in order to adjust the position.

The treatment is fundamentally very simple. All that is required is that *a double entry* should be made **for the amount involved** *reversing* the entry which was made when the goods were originally purchased.

EXAMPLE

Goods were bought on credit from P. Norman at a cost of £40 on 5th May.

P. Norman Account

	May 5 Purchase of Goods A/c	£40

Purchase of Goods Account

May 5 P. Norman A/c	£40	

Let us now suppose that £12 worth of these goods were returned to Norman on 9th May because they were defective. As was stated above, all that is needed is to *reverse* the entries set out above to the extent of the amount of goods returned, *i.e.* £12.

The *returns aspect only* would appear thus:

P. Norman Account

May 9	Purchase of	
	Goods A/c	£12

Purchase of Goods Account

	May 9 P. Norman A/c	£12

NOTE: The details of 5th May recording the original purchase of the goods has been omitted in the above entries so that the *effect* of returning goods to a supplier may be fully observed.

According to the last double entry above, Norman appears as a *debtor* for £12 but obviously we must combine *all* the entries in order to see the full picture. This would appear as follows:

P. Norman Account

May 9	Purchase of Goods A/c (returns)	£12	May 5	Purchase of Goods A/c (original purchase)	£40
9	Balance c/d	28			
		£40			£40
			May 9	Balance b/d	£28

Purchase of Goods Account

May 5	P. Norman A/c	£40	May 9	P. Norman A/c	£12
			9	Balance c/d	28
		£40			£40
May 9	Balance b/d	£28			

NOTE: In practice we do *not* balance off the Purchase of Goods

Account. It is only done here to tidy up the account and to show the *significant* figure of purchases.

The above example has been designed to show the *principle* involved. It is, of course, perfectly simple but most text books use an alternative presentation to deal with *the return of goods.* This alternative is perfectly sound, of course, but it does introduce an *additional* account. The *final* result is the same but makes for a slightly longer operation. Only one additional account is required but it is entitled either:

(*a*) Purchase Returns Account, or
(*b*) Returns **Outwards** Account.

EXAMPLE

On 3rd September goods costing £47 are bought from C. Medwin. Of these £9 worth were returned to him on 7th September. The original purchase would be recorded as follows:

C. Medwin Account

	Sept. 3 Purchase of Goods A/c £47

Purchase of Goods Account

Sept. 3 C. Medwin A/c £47	

On 7th September the following entries will be made:

C. Medwin Account

Sept. 7 **Purchase Returns A/c** (or Returns Outwards A/c) **£9**	Sept. 3 Purchase of Goods A/c £47

Purchase Returns Account or *Returns Outwards Account*

	Sept. 7 **C. Medwin A/c** **£9**

In this situation we have one account which deals with the *original* purchase of the goods (£47) and a *different* one for the re-

turn of part of that purchase (£9). Consequently, at the *end* of the
period of trading we will have to transfer *the total of the returns* to
the credit of the Purchase of Goods Account. The reason for
this is that the only *significant* amount we require in the Trading
Account is the amount of *goods actually purchased*. Goods
returned to the supplier are of no interest whatever.

6. Sales returns. When a *customer* returns goods to the seller
because he finds them defective or damaged, he must be given
credit for their value. The treatment in the ledger accounts is
similar to that employed with purchase returns but, of course,
in the opposite direction. Here we have the case of a sale which
has failed in whole or in part and, as a result, the position must
be adjusted.

EXAMPLE

Goods are sold on credit to S. Walters on 6th February for £60.

S. Walters Account

Feb. 6　Sales A/c	£60	

Sales Account

	Feb. 6　S. Walters A/c	£60

On 8th February Walters sends back some of the goods,
invoice value £15. Dealing with the *returns* aspect only we have:

S. Walters Account

	Feb. 8　Sales A/c	£15

Sales Account

Feb. 8　S. Walters A/c	£15	

Now combining *all* the entries the position would appear as
below:

S. Walters Account

Feb. 6	Sales A/c (original sale)	£60	Feb. 8	Sales A/c (returns)	£15
			8	Balance c/d	45
		£60			£60
Feb. 8	Balance b/d	£45			

Sales Account

Feb. 8	S. Walters A/c	£15	Feb. 6	S. Walters A/c	£60
8	Balance c/d	45			
		£60			£60
			Feb. 8	Balance b/d	£45

NOTE: As in the example dealing with purchases *we do not*, in practice, balance off the Sales Account. It is only done here to show the *final* figure of sales.

Very often a separate account is opened to deal with the return of goods sold. It is called either:

(*a*) Sales Returns Account, or
(*b*) Returns **Inwards** Account.

If such an account is used (under either title) it will be necessary at the end of the period of trading to close it off and *transfer the total* of all the returns to the *debit* of Sales Account.

7. Returns outwards and returns inwards. Most students, when they first study book-keeping, are apt to be confused by the terms "returns *outwards*" and "returns *inwards*" and frequently mix them up.

It is suggested that if you think of the word "outwards" as referring to something which you once possessed *but have now returned*, i.e. something which is going *away* from you or going *out of* the business, you will grasp its significance more readily and remember it permanently. After all, when you *return* goods, *i.e.* send back goods to the person from whom you bought them, the goods really *are* leaving you and going *out of* your possession. Hence the term "returns *outwards*."

The opposite, of course, is true of goods which a customer

returns *to* you. They come back *into* the business and so are called "returns inwards."

MISCELLANEOUS

8. A credit balance on a debtor's account. Sometimes we find a reference being made to the fact that there is a *credit* balance outstanding on the account of a *customer, i.e.* someone to whom we have *sold* goods. In normal circumstances we expect to find only *debit* balances on such accounts, for when a customer buys goods on credit his personal account will be *debited*. As a result there will ordinarily be a surplus of debits on his account which will only be cleared when he makes payment. Thus we normally expect to find debit balances *only* on customers' accounts.

It happens occasionally, however, that *after* the customer has paid for the goods and his account has, in consequence, been balanced off, he finds it necessary to *return* some of the goods. In such a case his account will be *credited* (and the Sales Account or Returns Inwards Account debited) with the value of the returned goods. The usual procedure on the part of the seller, particularly if the customer is a good one, is to ask him whether he wishes an immediate refund of cash to be made to him, or, alternatively, if he would prefer the *credit* to stand on his account and be set off against his next order. If he chooses the latter then we have the case of a credit balance standing on a debtor's account.

EXAMPLE

Goods were sold on credit to P. Baker for £85 on 17th March. He paid for the goods by cheque on 14th April but one week later on the 21st he returned goods to the value of £16 which had proved to be defective.

When the entries recording these matters have been made in P. Baker's ledger account it would appear as follows:

P. Baker Account

Mar. 17	Sales A/c	£85	Apr. 14	Bank A/c		£85
			Apr. 21	Returns Inwards A/c (or Sales A/c)		£16

Thus, on 21st April there is a *surplus* of credit over debit entries, *i.e.* there is a credit balance on a debtor's account.

9. Payment on account. Beginners sometimes ask what the position would be when a customer only pays a *portion* of the sum which he owes.

It is not uncommon for firms to have certain items under dispute at the time when normal monthly settlement of the account becomes due. In such circumstances many business houses make it a practice to pay that part of the account on which agreement has been reached, leaving payment of the disputed items in abeyance until matters have been settled to the satisfaction of both parties.

EXAMPLE

Goods to the value of £56 are sold to J. Greaves on 16th March. On 12th April, which is the usual monthly date on which Greaves pays his accounts, there is a query on an item of £19. Greaves therefore only pays that part of the transaction which has been passed for payment, *i.e.* £37. His account in the books of the seller would appear as follows:

J. Greaves Account

Mar. 16	Sales A/c	£56	Apr. 12	Bank A/c	£37
			Apr. 30	Balance c/d	19
		£56			£56
May 1	Balance b/d	£19			

10. A practical examination point. Many questions in book-keeping examinations give a trial balance and ask the candidate to prepare the Trading and Profit and Loss Account and a balance sheet. He is *not* asked to make entries in *the various ledger accounts*. The trial balance very often contains items for sales *returns* and purchases *returns* and in such cases the examinee is expected to show *each* of these returns items *as a deduction* from the sales and purchases, respectively, in the Trading Account.

PROGRESS TEST 9

Theory

1. What do you understand by the term "credit transaction"? (2)

2. What is the essential difference between cash transactions and credit transactions? (3)

3. In what way are these two types of transaction ultimately identical? (3)

4. What are the alternative names given to the accounts which deal with the return of goods (a) to the seller, and (b) by the purchaser? (5, 6)

5. How does a credit balance arise on a debtor's account? (8)

6. What do you understand by the expression "payment on account"? (9)

Practice

7. From the following information write up the ledger accounts concerned and then extract a trial balance.

Invoices received from suppliers, etc.:

May 4	J. Petry	goods	£47
9	W. Abbot	,,	102
12	T. Jackson	,,	91
17	L. Mears	office typewriter	75
23	P. Sanders	goods	148
29	H. French	repairs to office	125

Invoices sent to customers:

May 6	V. Lewis	goods	£63
8	K. Glover	,,	175
11	F. Harrison	,,	42
15	M. Wilkinson	,,	108
19	S. Gray	,,	31
23	B. Howell	,,	90
26	C. Kingsley	,,	54
30	D. Phillips	,,	17

During the month of June the following entries were made in the cash book (Bank Account):

Bank Account

June 1	Capital A/c	£450	June 9	J. Petry	£47
8	K. Glover (on account)	100	9	W. Abbot	102
20	M. Wilkinson	108	18	L. Mears	75
24	F. Harrison	42	30	H. French	125
29	B. Howell	90			

8. H. Clutterbuck opened a business on 1st May investing £1,500 which he paid into a bank account on this date. The following transactions took place during the month:

May	1	Paid one month's rent by cheque	30
	2	Bought goods on credit from T. Bradley	100
	3	Sold goods on credit to W. Rodgers	40
	6	Paid Bradley's account by cheque	100
	7	Drew cash from bank	25
	7	Paid wages in cash	18
	7	Cash sales	139
	10	Rodgers paid cash on account	20
	12	Bought goods from A. Scott on credit	275
	13	Cash purchases	5
	14	Cash sales	72
	14	Paid wages in cash	18
	16	Sold goods on credit to T. Williamson	115
	18	Paid sundry expenses in cash	11
	18	Paid cash into bank	50
	20	Paid stationery in cash	7
	21	Cash sales	64
	21	Paid wages in cash	18
	23	Paid cash into bank	40
	25	Paid insurance by cheque	22
	26	Sold goods to T. Naylor on credit	38
	28	Cash sales	71
	28	Paid wages in cash	18
	31	Paid Scott by cheque	275
	31	Drew cash for own use	80
	31	Paid all cash into bank except for £10	

Post the above transactions to the ledger. Take out a trial balance and then prepare the "final" accounts, *i.e.* the Trading Account and the Profit and Loss Account, showing the cost of sales and calculating the percentage of gross profit. Finally, construct a balance sheet to show the position on 31st May. (The closing stock at cost was valued at £80.)

9. (*a*) P. Lorrimer began business on 1st October with a capital of £500 which consisted of: cash at bank, £475; cash in hand, £25. The transactions which took place in the following fortnight were:

Oct.	7	Bought goods and paid by cheque	£200
	3	Bought goods from Farmer and Co.	250
	7	Cash sales paid into bank	70
	8	Paid Farmer and Co. by cheque	250
	10	Paid sundry expenses in cash	12
	12	Sold goods to D. Hughes	340
	14	Paid wages to assistant in cash	6

Prepare final accounts and balance sheet as at 15th October. (Stock at cost on 14th October was £170.)

(b) Continue the accounts for a further period.

Oct.	18	Bought goods from Farmer and Co.	£300
	20	Sold goods for cash	53
	22	Sold goods to E. Heath	200
	22	Paid carriage charges in cash	2
	22	D. Hughes paid on account by cheque	200
	24	Sold goods to E. Heath	136
	28	Paid assistant's wages in cash	6
	31	Paid one month's rent by cheque	48
	31	Paid cash into bank	40

The value of the closing stock at 31st October valued at cost was £190. Prepare the final accounts and balance sheet as at 31st October.

CHAPTER X

THE LEDGER AND ITS SUPPORTING BOOKS

1. The four main sections of the ledger. Up to this stage we have stressed the fact that in theoretical book-keeping *only one book is necessary*, and this remains true so far as the *theory* of book-keeping is concerned.

In practice, however, this state of affairs does not hold good except for any but the smallest business. As trade increases the work involved in recording transactions grows and with this growth it becomes necessary to break down the work into sections.

The first stage of this process of breaking down is to divide the ledger into *four* sections, as follows:

Section 1 contains the Bank Account only.

Section 2 contains the personal accounts of the creditors only.

Section 3 contains the personal accounts of the debtors only.

Section 4 contains the various expense accounts, asset accounts, the Capital Account of the owner, loan accounts (if any) and those few accounts which record items of income, *e.g.* Sales Account and Discount Received Account.

Each of these sections has a special name for itself. These are as follows:

Section 1: The Cash Book
Section 2: The Bought Ledger
Section 3: The Sales Ledger
Section 4: The Private Ledger.

It is as well at this point to call the student's attention to the fact that some of the titles mentioned above have certain *alternative* names, *e.g.* the Bought Ledger may be called the "Purchase Ledger" or "Creditors Ledger," while the "Sales Ledger" is sometimes referred to as the "Debtors Ledger" or "Sold Ledger." The Private Ledger is variously described as the "General Ledger," the "Nominal Ledger" or the "Impersonal Ledger." Sometimes the Private Ledger is used exclusively for the Capital Accounts, Loan Accounts and anything regarded as being completely confidential, and an extra book called the "General Ledger" is used for those accounts which ultimately appear in the Trading Account and the Profit and Loss Account.

In spite of these variations it is emphasised that *as far as this book is concerned* the four sections will be called the Cash Book, the Bought Ledger, the Sales Ledger and the Private Ledger.

One point of great importance which must always be remembered is that although we do, in fact, make use of these sections or divisions, each one *theoretically remains part of the ledger.* Furthermore, although we are making entries in these *subdivisions* the student must remember the basic fact of bookkeeping which is that *all* of the double entry must be made in the ledger, the whole of which is equal to the sum of all its parts.

BOOKS OF ORIGINAL ENTRY

2. The Day Books. At the same time as we subdivide the ledger into four sections it is appropriate to introduce some other books which, while *not forming a part of the double entry,* are nevertheless of considerable help in practice. These books are often referred to as "books of *original* entry" because the first record of many transactions is made in them.

The first of these is called the "Bought Day Book" and the second, the "Sales Day Book." Alternative names are the "Purchase" Day Book and the "Sold" Day Book. In addition to these two Day Books two others, called "Returns Day Books," are in common use, one for goods returned to suppliers and the other for goods returned by customers. These will be dealt with in some detail shortly.

The entries which are made in all of these Day Books originate from the invoices and credit notes as the case may be. Details from these documents are simply copied into the appropriate Day Book so that the business may have *a record in convenient form* of these particular transactions. These entries are *not part of the double entry*. They are a form of diary entry to serve as a reminder that the transactions which they represent have, in fact, taken place, and therefore *require processing, i.e.* that they must be recorded in double-entry form in two places in the ledger. (The appropriate section will, of course, depend upon their nature.)

3. Problems in recording credit transactions. When dealing with purely theoretical book-keeping we showed how, when goods were bought on credit, the double entry was made in the ledger by debiting the Purchase of Goods Account and crediting the account of the supplier. With only three or four credit transactions to be recorded this practice was quite straightforward especially when confined to simple exercises. However, in practice, there are disadvantages in operating in this manner.

Consider what would happen if we take a business of only modest size. Suppose that this firm obtained goods on credit from one hundred different suppliers and that, on the average, one transaction per month were conducted with each. This would give us 1,200 credit transactions in a year (the normal trading period of a business). It is usual to find that one page of a ledger will contain approximately 30 lines. This would mean that in one complete year forty pages would be needed in the ledger for the Purchase of Goods Account to be written up fully with the main details of every credit transaction. Forty pages for one single account is, without doubt, a lot.

One of the most important objectives of accountancy is that it should give information. What is equally important is that this information be given clearly and in a form which can be grasped quickly. A person who sat down to examine the ledger might well wonder, on looking through a Purchase of Goods Account forty pages long, when he was coming to the end of it before finding the information which he sought, *i.e. the total cost of goods purchased* during the year.

Consequently, some less detailed method of recording the above facts in the Purchase of Goods Account would be a big step forward. This is done, in fact, by introducing a *subsidiary* book which is called the "Bought Day Book" (or "Purchases Day Book").

4. The Bought Day Book. This is simply a *diary* and nothing more. The only information which needs to be recorded in it is:

(a) the *date* of the transaction,
(b) the *name* of the supplier and
(c) the *amount* of the purchase.

With this information given in the form of an entry in a diary we can make our posting *to the credit side* of the supplier's account and thus keep *a day-to-day check* on the position so far as each creditor is concerned. It is, of course, a matter of great importance to make sure that the business is not running up unduly high bills with its suppliers. Therefore, all purchases of goods which are entered in the Bought Day Book should be posted to the credit of the supplier's account *on the same day.* In this way we can avoid allowing matters to get out of control and eliminate the danger of excessive buying, for we must always remember that there is a *time limit* within which bills must be paid.

Every transaction must be entered in the ledger: once as a credit entry and once as a debit entry as we know. In the paragraph above we have dealt with the credit entry for each individual transaction. Now let us look at the corresponding debit entry. Here we depart temporarily from the strict rule of making both the debit and credit entries *at the same time.*

As has already been pointed out a very large number of pages would be required for the details to be entered in the Purchase of Goods Account if every individual transaction were to be debited thereto. So long as *the details* of the transactions have been recorded once, in the Bought Day Book, it would be pointless *to repeat them* all over again somewhere else in the business records, *i.e.* in the Purchase of Goods Account. Each single page of the Bought Day Book, therefore, is added up and the *total* of all the goods which have been purchased during the month is duly ascertained. This total is then entered on the *debit* side of the Purchase of Goods Account at *the end of the month, i.e. in one lump sum.*

In this way the precept of "every debit entry having its corresponding credit entry" is fulfilled, for it does not matter in normal circumstances if a certain amount of delay occurs in carrying out the rule. That the rule *is* carried out is the important thing.

An objection which is raised by some students is as follows: what happens if it becomes necessary to prepare accounts in a hurry at, say, some date in the middle of the month? In such a case, of course, the additions would be made in the Bought Day Book *at this date* and the necessary entry made in the Purchase of Goods Account, thus *completing* the double entry. In other words, it does not matter *at what date* the total is posted to the Purchase of Goods Account. We simply make it on the date which is convenient. The month end is generally regarded as the normally convenient time.

5. The Sales Day Book. The principle governing the use of the Sales Day Book is identical to that of the Bought Day Book.

This book, too, is simply a daily diary in which the essential details of the transaction are recorded. In this case the details are:

    (*a*) the *date* of the sale,
    (*b*) the *name* of the customer and
    (*c*) the *amount* of the sale.

It should be noted here that occasionally an unnecessary amount of detail is sometimes shown in illustrations of Day Books. It is a needless waste of time, effort and paper to write in the full details of the transaction, *e.g.* "6 Speedwell bicycles at £18 each." Those details will be shown fully on the *invoice*, a copy of which will always be kept. Reference may be made to this copy should the need arise. Consequently, it is unnecessary for details such as these to be *repeated* in the Day Books.

6. The Returns Books. It sometimes happens that for some reasons goods are returned to the firm which supplied them. The details of returned goods will be entered in special Returns Day Books, one for purchase returns and one for sales returns. Each item relating to returned goods, whether "inwards," *i.e.* coming back into the firm which sold them, or "outwards," *i.e.* going back to the supplier, will be posted *individually* to the *personal account* in the appropriate ledger. At the end of each month the respective Returns Day Books will be added up and the *total* for the month posted to the *debit* of the Sales Returns

Account with regard to returns inwards, and to the *credit* of the Purchases Returns Account with regard to returns outwards. In this way the double entry will be completed.

The rulings in these books are identical to those of the Sales and Bought Day Books. The method of entry is exactly the same also, the information entered being the *date* of the transaction, the *name* of the firm concerned and the *value* of the goods returned.

7. Rulings for Day Books and Returns Books. The rulings for the Day Books and Return Books are normally of a standard pattern and it is, therefore, most important that each of the books be clearly titled because if this is not done it may lead to considerable confusion in the office.

The standard ruling is as follows:

Date	Name of customer or of supplier	Ledger folio	Amount

This standard form of ruling can, if necessary, be adapted to the particular needs of a business. For example, some firms make a practice of entering an invoice number against each item. This can be done readily by ruling another column to the left of the folio column, for instance. Other firms may wish that "Purchase Tax" be shown against items should it apply to their business. Again, where a firm has a number of different departments it may wish to show items relating to each department separately. On the other hand, many firms will have separate Day Books for each department. From this it can be seen that there is a wide degree of flexibility with regard to the presentation of information. What may be perfect for one firm would be most unsatisfactory for another and so each firm will devise the system which suits its needs best.

The following examples will show the manner in which Day Books are used.

EXAMPLE

Goods were purchased by J. Snodgrass and were entered in the purchase day book as follows:

PURCHASE DAY BOOK

Date	Name of supplier	Bought ledger folio	Account
Apr. 4	F. Mason	M.27	£125
20	T. Cooper	C.39	14
22	A. Robinson	R.15	78
			£217

The postings in the Bought Ledger would be:

F. Mason Account

	Apr. 4 Purchase day book (or P.D.B.) £125

T. Cooper Account

	Apr. 20 P.D.B. £14

A. Robinson Account

	Apr. 22 P.D.B. £78

At the end of the month, *i.e.* on 30th April the *total* of the Purchase Day Book will be posted to the *debit* side of the Purchases Account in the Private Ledger.

Purchases Account

Apr. 30 Purchase Day Book £217	

In this way the double entry is completed.

EXAMPLE

Snodgrass sold goods on credit to certain customers during the month of May. From the *copy* invoices he made the following entries in the Sales Day Book:

SALES DAY BOOK

Date	Name of customer	Sales Ledger folio	Amount
May 1	J. MacHugh		£78
15	M. Wilkinson		144
26	C. Kingsley		69
			£291

NOTE: "Sales Ledger folio" in the third column refers to the *page* in the Sales Ledger which contains the *personal* account of the particular customer to which the item must be posted.

SALES LEDGER
J. MacHugh

May 1	Sales Day Book (or S.D.B.)	£78	

M. Wilkinson

May 15	S.D.B.	£144	

C. Kingsley

May 26	S.D.B.	£69	

At the end of the month, *i.e.* on 31st May, the *total* amount of the *credit* sales (£291) will be posted to the *credit* side of the Sales Account in the Private Ledger direct from the sales day book.

PRIVATE LEDGER

Sales Account

		May 31	Sales day book £291

Thus we see that each of the three *personal* accounts is debited with its appropriate item *on the date when the transaction took place*. The double entry is *not completed* until the *end* of the month when Sales Account is credited with a lump sum, *i.e.* the total of all the individual sales on credit.

The entries in each of the two *Returns* Day Books will be dealt with on exactly the same principle. The total of the Purchase Returns Book will be credited to Purchase Returns Account, each item having been debited *individually* to the appropriate personal account. In like manner the total of the Sales Returns Book will be debited to Sales Returns Account, personal accounts each being credited with the individual item with which it is concerned.

ANALYSED DAY BOOKS

8. The purpose of analysed Purchase Day Books. A further variation employed by some firms is the use of a Purchase Day Book containing a number of analysis columns. This type of Day Book is employed where a firm wishes to maintain a personal account in the Bought Ledger with regard to the various services of which it makes use, *e.g.* telephone, advertising, electricity, etc. When invoices for these various services are received they are entered in the analysed Purchase Day Book along with all the invoices received from suppliers of goods. If the standard form of Day Book ruling were used, all invoices coming into the firm, no matter to what they refer, would be entered in the money column. Since they would not all represent goods purchased for resale it would be useless debiting the total to the Purchases Account because, before we were able to prepare the final accounts, we would have to analyse the total and post the results to the various expense accounts.

If an *analysed* Purchase Day Book is used, each item, whether it be for goods or for services, will first have to be entered in a "total" column. It will then be *extended*, *i.e.* repeated, in one of the various analysis columns to the right of the total column. At the end of each month all the columns would be added up or "cast." The total column would contain *every item* and the total of all the analysis columns would, if correctly cast, be equal to the amount shown in the total column. Thus, by "cross-casting" (*i.e.* adding across the columns), the analysis columns and ensuring that the *total* of these agrees with the total column, we can be satisfied that everything is in order. The total of *each* analysis column is then posted to the debit side of the appropriate nominal account in the Private Ledger.

EXAMPLE

During the month of May a firm wrote up its analysed Purchase Day Book as follows:

ANALYSED PURCHASE DAY BOOK

Date	Name	Folio	Total	Pur-chases	Light and heat	Rent and rates	Tele-phone	Insur-ance
May 4	P. Dixon		£30	£30				
6	F. Hewson		48	48				
8	S.X. Elec. Bd.		17		£17			
11	H. Law—rent		250			£250		
13	S. Adams		22	22				
15	T. Williams—insurance		36					£36
18	K. Kingsley Ltd.		109	109				
21	Telephone Co.		15				£15	
22	S.X. Gas Company		8		8			
26	S.X. Council—rates		87			87		
28	D. Lines & Co.		269	269				
			£891	£478	£25	£337	£15	£36

The total column amounts to £891. The cross-cast of the analysis columns also amounts to £891 and so we can be satisfied that the analysis is correct.

Each item entered in the total column would be posted to the *credit side* of the appropriate personal account in the Bought Ledger. At the end of the month the *total* of each of the analysis columns would be posted to the *debit* side of an account bearing the name of its respective column, thus completing the double entry. So if we considered the invoices in respect of rent and rates the entries in the Bought Ledger would appear as under:

H. Law Account

	July 11　Purchase Day Book	£250

S.X. Council Account

	May 26　Purchase Day Book	£87

At the end of May the *total* of the "Rent and Rates" column in the analysed Purchase Day Book would be posted *in one sum* to the *debit* of the nominal account of that name in the Private Ledger.

Rent and Rates Account

May 31 P.D.B.	£337	

This pattern would be followed for all the other entries in the analysed Purchase Day Book.

9. Invoices and the Bought Ledger. It is important for the student to realise that when an "analysed" Purchase Day Book is used *every single invoice*, whether it be for goods (to resell) or for services (such as the telephone), will have to be credited to a *personal* account in the Bought Ledger. When the bills are paid the credit entry will appear in the Cash Book (Bank Account) and the corresponding debit in the personal account in the Bought Ledger. In this manner the various creditors' accounts will be "closed off" and we will be left with the nominal account (in the above example, the Rent and Rates Account) showing as a debit the full *charge*. This will ultimately be transferred to the Profit and Loss Account.

PROGRESS TEST 10

Theory

1. Into how many sections is the ledger subdivided? What are the names of the respective sections and what accounts do they contain? **(1)**

2. What is a Day Book? What are Day Books used for? **(2)**

3. Write a short note on the purpose of the Bought Day Book and describe the manner in which this purpose is achieved. **(3, 4)**

4. How are returned goods dealt with? **(6)**

5. What basic information must be entered in the Day Books? How are the principles of double entry satisfied? **(4, 7)**

Practice

6. Open a Purchase Day Book on the analysis principle and enter the following items therein. All items are to be regarded as *credit* transactions.

April 1	Bought goods from N. Rees	£10
3	Invoice from Exton Electricity Board received	32
4	Received demand for General Rates from Exton Borough Council	84
5	Bought goods from B. Connor	27

8	Received invoice from Baker Bros, for stationery	15
9	Invoice for purchase of coal received from Charlton & Co.	58
10	Bought goods from L. Perkins Ltd.	109
12	,, ,, ,, J. Millington	22
13	Exton Gas Board sent in account	41
16	Lincoln & Sons rendered account for insurance premium	28
17	Bought goods from Clay & Co. Ltd.	89
19	Sinclair Ltd. sent in invoice for advertising	34
20	A. Landlord's invoice for three months' rent received	120
23	Bought goods from Fielding & Co.	65
24	Exton Garage Ltd. sent bill for motor repairs	23
25	Received demand from Post Office for telephone charges	29
26	Invoice received from Office Supplies Co. for new typewriter	95
28	Exton Press Ltd. rendered account for headed notepaper	14
29	Received invoice for repairs to machinery from L. Harrington	38
30	Bought goods from S. Neil	55
30	Exton Garage Ltd. sent in bill for petrol	17

CHAPTER XI

DISCOUNTS

THE USE OF INCENTIVES

1. What the term "discount" means to a businessman. In the context of business transactions, *"discount"* means *"incentive."* By this we mean that a form of bribery is put into operation, the object of which is to persuade people to pay their bills more speedily than they might otherwise do.

The incentive offered to the customer usually takes the form of a promise by the creditor to accept *less than the full amount* of the debt due provided that payment is made within a specified period of time. Thus goods may be sold on stated terms such as "Terms—5% 30 days." This means that the supplier is prepared to accept 95 per cent of the price at which the goods were *invoiced* to the customer so long as the purchaser makes payment within 30 days of the date of the statement. Let us say, for example, that Clutterbuck bought goods from Snodgrass for £60 on terms which offered him a discount of 5 per cent provided payment was made within 30 days. If Clutterbuck settled the account within the stipulated time, Snodgrass would be satisfied to receive £57 in full settlement of the amount due.

In business we meet with two different types of discount: (*a*) trade discount and (*b*) cash discount.

2. Trade discount. Discounts of this nature will not concern us in this book. At the same time, however, it is right that the reader should understand what is meant by the term.

Trade discounts are allowances which the seller deducts *before* invoicing his customer. Thus when the customer receives the invoice from his supplier any *deduction* for trade discount will already have been made. The buyer will therefore enter the *net* amount of the invoice in his ledger, *i.e.* to the credit of the supplier's account and (ultimately by means of the Bought Day Book) to the debit of the Purchase of Goods Account.

The particular reason why the supplier made the allowance

will be of no special interest to the buyer. All that he is concerned about is how much money he will have to pay for the goods.

3. Reasons for the use of trade discount. There may be a number of reasons why a supplier employs the use of trade discounts when dealing with his customers. For example, it not infrequently happens that a powerful retailer with, say, a large number of branches, may be offered goods at a somewhat lower price than that offered to small customers.

EXAMPLE

Snodgrass Stores Ltd. has a chain of fifty branches. It purchases a particular line of goods from Todhunter & Co. Ltd. The goods cost Todhunter £1 each. These are marked up to a selling price of £1·50 per item and are sold to the *majority* of customers at that figure. Snodgrass Stores with its fifty branches is a very attractive selling outlet, however, and provided that it purchases a stipulated minimum number of articles each year, a selling price of £1·40 per item is agreed upon. This is a trade discount.

Accordingly, when the goods are invoiced the cost to Snodgrass Stores Ltd. for 10,000 items, say, would amount to £14,000. Suppose that one hundred smaller customers had each purchased one hundred items they would have been invoiced individually at £1·50 each for, *i.e.* a total of £150 per customer. This would have amounted to a sale price of £15,000 in all, as compared with £14,000 for the same quantity sold to Snodgrass Stores Ltd.

It can be seen, therefore, that *no* trade discount applies to the smaller customers.

When payment was made in due course the amounts would be as shown above which is to say that payment would be made on *the amount invoiced*. This is the *vital* amount which is credited to the supplier's account in each buyer's books. So far as the accountant of Snodgrass Stores Ltd. is concerned all he knows is that he has to credit Todhunter's account with £1·40 per item and to pay on that amount. The smaller firms only know that the cost to them is £1·50 and that payment at that rate per item has to be made.

CASH DISCOUNTS

4. Cash discount. The possession or control of money is of tremendous importance in business. The ownership of funds in any quantity places a very strong lever in the hands of its

ossessor since he can supply it in any way which he considers
ᴉay be to his advantage.

When a businessman sells goods *on credit* he is actually
ꬶnancing his customer during the period in which the bill
ᴇmains unpaid. Suppose A bought goods at a cost of £80 and
ᴏld them on credit to B for £100. Until B pays the bill for
ᴉ00, A is out of pocket to the extent of £80, the amount which
ᴇ, at an earlier date, had to pay for the goods. In such circum-
ᴛances he is unable to use his £80 since it is out of his control
ᴏr the time being. If he can persuade B to pay him without
ᴉndue delay he could make use of his £80 *together with the profit
ꬶ £20* and buy a fresh supply of goods, and thereby hope to
ᴇll these also at a profit.

In the hope of persuading B to pay him quickly he therefore
ꞏffers him a *cash discount* of, say, 5 per cent. In other words
ᴀ is prepared to *reduce his margin of profit* from £20 to £15
ꞏecause the sooner he receives his money the sooner he will be
ꞏble to purchase a fresh supply of goods and make a fresh sale,
ᴛhus earning an additional amount of profit.

5. The two kinds of cash discount. Cash discounts fall into
ᴛwo categories: (*a*) discounts allowed, and (*b*) discounts
ᴇceived.

The term "discounts allowed" is used to denote cash dis-
ᴄount *offered to customers* and duly taken by them, *i.e.* when
ᴛhey pay their bills within the customary time-limit (the
ᴉumber of days allowed may vary slightly between one trade
ᴉnd another).

EXAMPLE

Wilson sells goods to Peter Brown for £200 on 15th May and
offers him a discount of 2·5 per cent provided payment is made
on or before 15th June. Brown settles his account on 10th June
and deducts £5 (2·5 per cent of £200).

The entries to be made in Wilson's ledger accounts would be:

Peter Brown Account

May 15	Sales A/c	£200	June 10	Bank A/c	£195
			10	**Discount Allowed A/c**	5
		£200			£200

Discount Allowed Account

June 10	**Peter Brown A/c**	£5

NOTE: The entries in the Sales Account and Bank Account have been ignored in this illustration.

The term "discount received" is used in connection with the settlement of a creditor's account, *i.e.* when *payment is being made* for goods which have been *purchased* by a business. When we speak of "discount received" we do not mean that money has been received; the expression simply means that our creditors have accepted *less* money than the amount to which they were entitled and, into the bargain, have agreed that the debts due are considered to have been settled *in full*. The effect of this arrangement on the finances of the debtor, *i.e.* the person making the payment, is exactly the same as if he had, in fact, *received money*.

EXAMPLE

David Jenkins purchased goods from William French for £100 on 29th April. French promised to give him a discount of 3 per cent if he settled his account by 29th May. Jenkins paid his bill on 26th May and deducted £3. The entries to be made in Jenkins' ledger were:

William French Account

May 26	Bank A/c	£97	Apr. 29	Purchase of Goods A/c	£100
26	**Discount Received A/c**	3			
		£100			£100

Discount Received Account

			May 26	**William French A/c**	£3

NOTE: The entries in the Purchase of Goods Account and in the Bank Account have been ignored in this illustration.

THE MEMORANDUM COLUMNS

6. Memorandum columns for discount. The *basic* double
entries for discounts allowed and discounts received have been
shown in the two previous examples. In a business which had
many transactions of a credit nature this method would, in
practice, be rather cumbersome. It might well mean the
making of scores of *individual entries* in the Discount Allowed
Account and the Discount Received Account, filling up many
pages of the Private (or General) Ledger. To overcome this
difficulty it is usual to have a *special* column on the credit side
of the Cash Book (Bank Account) wherein discounts received
are recorded, while on the debit side, in another special column,
the discounts allowed are entered. These special columns are
not part of the double entry. They are known as "memorandum columns" and are used for convenience.

When an account is paid *the amount of the cheque* will be
entered on the credit side of the Cash Book (Bank Account),
e.g. £97 paid to William French in the last example. The discount received, £3, would be entered *on the same line, i.e. level*
with the £97 in the *memorandum column* and the *two* amounts
would be posted to the debit of William French's account.
Frequently in practice they are added together and the entry
would read "Cash and Discount £100." The object of this is to
save time and space. *No entry* is made in the Discount Received
Account at this stage.

This process is followed throughout the month and we are
left, *temporarily*, with the double entry in an *unfinished* con-
dition. However, at the end of the month the memorandum
column is added up and its *total, i.e.* all the amounts of discount
received, is then *credited* to the Discount Received Account.
This, of course, completes the double entry so far as these discounts are concerned. When this is done on a monthly basis it
means that at the end of the year the Discount Received
Account will have only twelve items (the twelve monthly
totals) standing to its credit with the resulting saving of a great
amount of space as well as a vast quantity of entries which in
this context are of comparatively little significance.

The same pattern is followed with regard to discounts
allowed. That is to say, on the debit side of the Cash Book
(Bank Account) again we will have a memorandum column,
this one containing information on the individual amounts of

discounts which have been *allowed* to customers. The process of posting the amounts of money received plus the discounts allowed will be identical to that used for the payments plus discounts received, except, of course, that in this case they will be *credited* in the customers' personal accounts.

EXAMPLE

J. Snodgrass entered into a number of transactions during the month of September. He bought goods on credit as follows:

Sept. 12	From H. Burrows	£200
16	C. Knowles	80
21	L. Harrison	140
26	R. Thurston	60
27	D. Baker	100

By arrangement with his suppliers he was entitled to deduct 5 per cent discount provided that he made payment within 30 days. He paid each of his creditors within the time limit allowed.

The entries in the Cash Book will be as illustrated below. Note particularly that the entries in the Discount Received column have been shown in *italic* type as a reminder that these items, as they stand in the Cash Book, are *not* to be regarded as being part of the double entry. *Individually*, each item is debited to the supplier's personal account in the ledger. At the end of the month the *total* of the column will be credited to the Discount Received Account.

CASH BOOK **(Credit side)**

Date	Details	Discount received (Memorandum)	Bank A/c
Oct. 10	H. Burrows	*£10*	£190
14	C. Knowles	*4*	76
20	L. Harrison	*7*	133
24	R. Thurston	*3*	57
27	D. Baker	*5*	95
		£29	£551

The reader is reminded that the accounts of the respective suppliers would have been *debited* with the appropriate amounts, *e.g.* H. Burrows £190 + £10 = £200, etc. The Discount Received Account would be *credited* with the month's total of £29, thus completing the double entry.

Discounts Received Account

	Oct. 31 Sundry Discounts (or "Sundries") £29

NOTE: The entry in the Discounts Received Account is often referred to as "Sundries." This is a term in general use indicating that *several* items are included. This term is often used in relation to matters other than discounts.

So that there can be no possibility of confusion let us examine a short example in respect of discounts *allowed*.

EXAMPLE

P. Cleghorn sold goods on credit as follows:

June 4	To B. Henderson	£75
9	M. Parker	125
17	S. Allen	50
22	D. Barnes	200
26	W. Wallis	100

Cleghorn had offered his customers a discount of 4 per cent for payment within 30 days. Each one took advantage of this offer.

CASH BOOK   **(Debit side)**

Date	Details	*Discount allowed* (Memorandum)	*Bank A/c*
July 2	B. Henderson	£3	£72
8	M. Parker	5	120
14	S. Allen	2	48
19	D. Barnes	8	192
25	W. Wallis	4	96
		£22	£528

The respective customers' accounts would have been *credited* with the appropriate sums, *e.g.* B. Henderson, £72 + £3 = £75, etc. The Discount Allowed Account would be *debited* at the end of the month with the total of £22. In this way the double entry would be completed.

Discount Allowed Account

July 31	Sundry discounts	£22	

7. Discounts allowed and discounts received in the final accounts. At the end of the trading year the respective discount accounts will be closed off and transferred to the Profit and Loss Account. Never, *in any circumstances*, should they be transferred to the Trading Account. *Marks will certainly be lost* in an examination if this is done.

This may seem strange at first sight because the seller, as a direct result of granting a discount, will suffer a *reduction* of his profit. Students tend to think, quite understandably, that it is the gross profit which ought to suffer the reduction since the discount is clearly bound up with the buying and selling of goods. They argue that **returned** goods are deducted from purchases or sales, so why should not discounts also be deducted.

The view is taken, however, that *returns* must be deducted from purchases and sales because, in effect, these were "*non*-transactions." If goods were sold for £100 and were then *returned* by the customer the net amount of the "sale" would be nil. Hence the use of the term "non-transaction."

Discounts, on the other hand, are really *additional* transactions to the main one. The taking of a discount might be called a "sub-transaction" since it is indeed linked with the original one. The real point is that the taking of a discount by the customer—remember that the purchaser of goods is a *customer* of the seller—is an entirely *optional* matter and will depend upon *the financial circumstances* of the person making the payment at that particular time. If he were making another payment two months afterwards in settlement of a later transaction he might not be in a position to take advantage of the discount offered. Because of the danger of this lack of consistency in discount transactions, they are *always* placed in the Profit and Loss Account so that the gross profit will not be affected and the calculation of the percentage of gross profit to sales may always be made upon a *consistent* basis.

PROGRESS TEST 11

Theory

1. What is meant by a note on an invoice which reads "Terms—5% 30 days"? **(1)**

2. What are the usual types of discount? **(1)**

3. What are "trade" discounts? **(2)**

4. How does a trade discount operate? **(3)**

5. Describe the workings of cash discount and state what benefits may accrue. **(4)**

6. There are two kinds of cash discount. State the name of each. **(5)**

7. Explain how the memorandum columns for discount received and discount allowed are operated. **(6)**

Practice

8. On 1st October W. Thomas was owed the following amounts:

J. Fleming	£67·20
T. Murphy	82·00
T. Maloney	149·00
I. Lines	75·00

Each of these receivable amounts was subject to a cash discount of 5 per cent if paid within a stated time limit, *i.e.* not later than 20th October. They were all paid on 18th October and the discount was duly taken. Show the entries in the Cash Book and the Sales Ledger assuming that there were no other entries during the month. Complete the double entry in the Private Ledger on 31st October.

9. It was the practice of G. Ellis to settle his accounts monthly and he paid his creditors regularly on the 26th of each month, taking 4 per cent discount. On 1st November he owed the following:

T. Duncan	£88·00
W. Creigh	46·00
B. Martin	115·00
M. O'Gara	63·75

Assuming that there were no other transactions during the month make the necessary entries in the Cash Book and the Bought Ledger. Complete the double entry in respect of discounts in the Private Ledger on 30th November.

CHAPTER XII

THE TRIAL BALANCE AND ITS LIMITATIONS

THE BUILD-UP OF THE TRIAL BALANCE

1. The basic purpose of the trial balance. The "check," which should always be made, on the correctness of the postings in the ledger, is known as the "Trial Balance." This was introduced in Chapter VI where its function was discussed.

We must remember that the *essential* preliminary to the preparation of the Trading and Profit and Loss Accounts and balance sheet is to ensure that the books are "in balance," *i.e.* that the double entry has been properly carried out and that all additions in the various accounts have been made correctly. This is done by preparing a Trial Balance.

2. Extracting a trial balance. An ordered routine should be followed when taking out a Trial Balance. The ledger is, as we know, the basic book in use. We also know that it is, for convenience, broken down into a number of sub-divisions, *i.e.* the Cash Book, the Bought Ledger, the Sales Ledger and the Private Ledger.

The "ordered routine" mentioned above to be followed in the preparation of a Trial Balance might well start with the Cash Book and then deal with the debtors and the creditors before coming to the Private Ledger. The reason for this suggested sequence is that the first three sub-divisions of the ledger can be organised in such a way that one single entry in the Trial Balance for each sub-division is all that is necessary. This leaves the Private Ledger as the one section which will have more than one item appearing in the Trial Balance.

3. The "ordered routine" to be followed. In the first place we should "balance off" the Cash Book *after checking it in detail* with the bank statements and reconciling it therewith. The balance on the Petty Cash Book should also be checked and verified as being correct. When these tasks have been performed *both balances* should be entered in the Trial Balance.

Attention must now be turned to the Bought Ledger. Each account should be "closed off" and any balances "carried down." The normal practice is for each separate balance to be entered on a "Schedule of Bought Ledger balances." This is done by examining each supplier's account, ensuring that the additions have been made correctly and that any balance has been properly entered and carried down to the next trading period. This balance should then be entered on the schedule of balances for that particular ledger. When the complete list of balances has been compiled the *total* should be entered in the Trial Balance.

Turning to the Sales Ledger we follow the same pattern, this time listing the customers' individual balances in a "Schedule of Sales Ledger balances." These will finally be totalled and *the sum total* entered in the Trial Balance.

There are now four items entered in the Trial Balance:

 (a) the bank balance;
 (b) the petty cash balance;
 (c) the creditors' balances *in one lump sum*, and
 (d) the debtors' balances *in one lump sum*.

The only section of the ledger not dealt with so far is the Private Ledger. It is a comparatively simple task to deal with this but it must be remembered that the balance on every single account in the Private Ledger *must* be extracted and *entered on its own* in the Trial Balance. There is no question here of any "schedule" of balances for the Private Ledger.

THE LIMITATIONS OF THE TRIAL BALANCE

4. Sequence of checks to be followed if a trial balance does not agree. It is quite a normal experience, in practice at least, to find that a Trial Balance does not agree. If the Trial Balance is "out," *i.e.* out of agreement, then obviously, an error has occurred somewhere. Where do we start to look for the mistake? It has already been suggested that, when a Trial Balance is being prepared we should follow an ordered sequence in building it up. Similarly, when a Trial Balance "disagrees," an ordered sequence should be followed in an effort to trace the difference. The sequence should be as logical as possible, although it may not be easy to decide which are the priorities. It is imperative, however, for the check to be thorough, otherwise we have no idea as to where the error or errors arose in the first place.

Probably the best method is to work "backwards" from the Trial Balance. If the first point does not reveal the difference then proceed to the second point and so on.

(*a*) Check the additions of *each side* of the Trial Balance.

(*b*) Check *each balance into* the Trial Balance from the various ledgers and cash books making sure that:

(*i*) no balance has been *omitted*;

(*ii*) each ledger balance has been placed *on its correct side* in the Trial Balance, and,

(*iii*) that *the figure entered* in the Trial Balance is the *same* as the figure in the ledger *e.g.* that no transposition of figures has been made.

(*c*) Verify that both the Bought Ledger and Sales Ledger balances have been proved *correct* by means of Control Accounts where these are in operation.

(*d*) The bank balance and petty cash balance should have been checked under (*ii*) above.

(*e*) We are now left with the Private Ledger "unproved." *Check each posting* into the various Private Ledger accounts and then *check the additions* of every account.

Apart from working to a pattern as suggested above other ideas on procedure will come as experience is gained. For instance, it is a good idea when making additions to add from the bottom upwards and, when checking, to add from the top downwards. Another useful hint, should the Trial Balance not agree, is to ascertain the amount of the difference and halve it, then look in the Trial Balance for either of the figures so revealed. For instance, if the Trial Balance should show a difference of £20, the *excess* being on the *credit* side, this could have been caused by an item of £10 being placed in the credit column instead of the debit column.

5. Errors and their effect on the trial balance. The fact that a Trial Balance agrees is prima facie proof that everything has been correctly dealt with in the books. Unfortunately, this impression can be misleading.

A Trial Balance which has been agreed will not disclose the following errors:

(*a*) Errors of *omission, e.g.* when an invoice is lost before being entered in the books. This will have *no effect* on the Trial Balance.

(*b*) Errors of *commission*, *e.g.* the posting of *the correct amount* to the *wrong account* as where a sale of, say, £25 which should have been debited to J. White (London) Ltd. but was, by mistake, debited to the account of J. White (Luton) Ltd. An error of this type would not affect the Trial Balance.

(*c*) Errors of *principle* as where, for example, the *purchase* of a second-hand motor van was debited to the Motor Expenses (Repairs) Account. This would be a case of treating an item of *capital* expenditure as a *revenue* expense. Such an error would *not* affect the agreement of the Trial Balance because the debit/credit treatment has been carried out (although the debit has been posted to the wrong account).

(*d*) *Compensating* errors. The effect of one mistake may be cancelled by a second mistake, of the same amount, being made on the opposite side of the ledger.

The Trial Balance would *not* disclose these errors even when the balance has been agreed.

PROGRESS TEST 12

Theory

1. What is the basic purpose of the Trial Balance? (**1**)
2. Set out in detail an orderly programme which should be followed when taking out a Trial Balance. (**2, 3**)
3. If a Trial Balance does not agree what checks would you carry out in order to ascertain where the error or errors lay? (**4**)
4. Make a list of the various kinds of errors which can occur in book-keeping. (**5**)

Practice

5. Prepare a Trial Balance from the list of balances set out below.

Capital	£1,420
Drawings	1,029
Furniture and fittings	82
Opening stock	647
Purchases	6,451
Sales	10,019
Rent and rates	683
Salaries	1,745
General expenses	627
Debtors	175

6. Prepare a Trial Balance at 30th June from the list of balances set out below. (In order to balance you must insert the amount of "capital" which has not been given.)

Bank	£724
Cash	18
Debtors	1,214
Creditors	1,467
Drawings	1,680
Opening stock	951
Office equipment	249
Motor vehicle	442
General expenses	1,190
Salaries and wages	2,479
Purchases	17,681
Sales	25,419
Rent	1,000
Rates and insurance	264
Telephone	53
Closing stock	1,066

After agreeing the Trial Balance prepare a Trading Account, a Profit and Loss Account and a balance sheet.

7. P. Harrison took out a Trial Balance from his business books as at 31st December 19–0, as follows:

Capital		£1,960
Drawings	£2,360	
Sales		24,801
Purchases	16,189	
Purchase returns		404
Stock at 1st January 19–0	2,462	
Shop equipment	941	
Debtors	2,279	
Creditors		2,714
Packing materials	265	
Rent and rates	839	
Light and heat	468	
Postage and telephone	127	
Insurances	48	
Wages	1,580	
Cash in hand	21	
Cash at bank	2,399	
	£29,978	£29,879

As the Trial Balance did not agree Harrison checked through his books and discovered the following errors:

(*a*) A bill for electricity, £33, for his private house had been charged to the Light and Heat Account of the business.

(*b*) A credit balance on a customer's account in the sales ledger amounting to £33 had been entered as a debit balance on the schedule of debtors and taken to the Trial Balance.

(*c*) The total for the month of May in the sales day book had been undercast by £50.

(*d*) Discounts given by a supplier had been correctly entered in the bought ledger but had been omitted from the Discounts Received Account. The amount was £14.

(*e*) A bad debt of £31 had been correctly entered in the Sales Ledger Account but had not been entered in the Bad Debts Account.

Make the adjustments necessary and rewrite the Trial Balance.

CHAPTER XIII

CAPITAL AND REVENUE

1. Classifying expenditure and income. In accounting all *expenditure* is classified under one of two headings:

(*a*) Expenditure of a *capital* nature, and
(*b*) Expenditure of a *revenue* nature.

In the same way *income* is treated as being either of a *capital* nature or of a *revenue* nature.

2. Altering the form of the original investment. We know that the one essential requirement of a business is *capital* and we know, too, that this is usually supplied in the form of *money*.

It is only when there are *goods or services available* in exchange that money assumes a value. Thus when a business is brought into existence and money is invested in it the money is of value only for what it will buy. At the start of its life a business will need various types of equipment as well as a stock of goods to enable it to commence trading. The money which it possesses, *i.e.* that which the *owner* has invested in it, will be used to supply these *initial* wants. That is to say, it will be used to put the business into a position *to start trading*.

It must be clearly understood that at this stage *no trading has taken place*. What has happened simply is that most of the money has been *exchanged* for goods which are to be sold and for shop equipment which is essential for carrying on the business. In other words, where in the first place the *only* asset possessed by the business was money, we now find that the *form* of this asset has been very largely changed but that *the total of the assets*, in terms of money, *still remains at the original figure* of the cash which was invested in the business.

EXAMPLE

On 1st January H. Nicholls invested £2,000 in a new business which was paid into an account with Barclays Bank.

Position on 1st January

Liabilities	H. Nicholls—Capital A/c	£2,000
Assets	Barclays Bank A/c	£2,000

On 4th January a motor van costing £750 was purchased and on 5th January shop fittings were bought for £600. In each case payment was made immediately.

Position on 5th January

Liabilities	H. Nicholls—Capital A/c		£2,000
Assets	Motor Van A/c	£750	
	Shop Fittings A/c	600	
	Barclays Bank A/c	650	
		———	£2,000

We can see that although the *form* of the investment has been altered—from one of *cash* (at Barclays Bank) *and nothing else* to an investment consisting of (*a*) a motor van, (*b*) shop fittings, and (*c*) some cash at Barclays Bank—the *total* of the *original* investment of £2,000 has *not* varied from that figure.

CAPITAL EXPENDITURE

3. The nature of capital expenditure. The purchase of an asset is referred to as "buying on capital account." The term "on capital account" in this context must not be confused with the owner's "Capital Account." When the asset is *bought* no entry will be made in the Capital Account of the owner. The spending of money in the purchase of fixed assets, *i.e.* things of a *permanent* nature, is called "*capital expenditure*," and this term would apply, in the example in **2** above, to the purchase of the motor van and shop fittings.

Once the Capital Account of the owner has been credited with the amount of his investment no entries will ever be made in this account with regard to the *spending* of the money invested. The money has been given to the banker to be looked after and in the business records the Bank Account will have been debited with this sum. If any of it is spent such spending will be recorded in the form of credit entries in the Bank Account. If the "Position on 5th January" is studied this fact will be quite clear. What has obviously happened is that money has been taken out of the care of Barclays Bank and given respectively: (a) to somebody who owned a motor van and (b) to somebody who owned shop fittings. *In return for the payment* of money these items have been transferred to the ownership of the business. This new state of affairs is reflected in the "Position on 5th January."

REVENUE EXPENDITURE

4. The nature of revenue expenditure. This term is used to refer to those *day-to-day expenses* which are unavoidable in the running of a business and which, therefore, *must* affect the profit earned. For example, if Nicholls had to pay wages to an assistant the effect of such a payment would be to reduce the profit. In exactly the same way if Nicholls had to pay rent for the use of his business premises this too would have to be set against his profit. From these two examples we can conclude that all items of revenue expenditure will *reduce* the profit. In most cases it is the Profit and Loss Account which will be debited with revenue expenditure, although in certain cases the Trading Account will bear the charge.

It should be quite clear that, as is shown in the example above, items of capital expenditure do *not* affect the profit. Such expenditure is simply a *redisposition* of the assets possessed by the business.

NOTE: Items of capital expenditure must never be debited in the Profit and Loss Account.

5. Purchases of goods for resale. The question of the purchase of goods for resale is a matter which calls for some clarification. (This particular activity also has such descriptions applied to it as "Purchases" or "Buying goods for stock.")

In the case of a *new* business part of the original cash invested will certainly be spent on "stocking" the shop, *i.e.* buying goods for resale. If we apply the principles laid down above we would decide that *in the opening stages* this should be treated as capital expenditure, since cash is being exchanged for an asset of *the same value* but of *a different nature*. There is, however, a difference *in purpose* between the purchase of goods for resale and the purchase, for example, of shop fittings. The shop fit-

ings are being bought so that the shop may be properly
quipped for the display and sale of goods. They are being
ought in the expectation that they will be *kept* for a number
f years and not with the intention of being sold at a profit.
he purchase of goods for resale, on the other hand, has been
ade with the sole objective of their being sold at a profit
t *the very first opportunity.*

It is conventional to regard *the purchase of goods for resale* as
n item of revenue expenditure.

In the interests of strict accuracy, however, it must be made
lear that although we find the item "Purchases" debited in the
rading Account, it should not be regarded on its own. It
hould always be read in conjunction with the opening stock
nd the closing stock. As we have seen already "gross profit"
s obtained by finding the difference between the cost of those
oods which have been sold and the price obtained from the
ale of those *same* goods. It should be evident, therefore, that
he item to be debited in the Trading Account is not simply the
Purchase of goods" but the "Cost of goods sold."

Let us now study an example in order to appreciate the
espective significance of capital expenditure and revenue
xpenditure.

EXAMPLE

K. McDonald commenced business on 1st January investing
£6,000 in a business. This money was paid into Barclays Bank.
Before starting trading the following transactions were completed:

Shop premises were bought for £3,250, shop fittings for
£1,200, a motor van for £540 and goods for resale for £800. All of
these items were paid for immediately by cheque.

After *equipping the business* as set out above McDonald
commenced trading during the month of February. The
following details summarise the events which took place:

By 28th February payment had been made by cheque for

Purchase of additional goods for resale	£400
Light and heat	5
Insurance	2
Wages	40
Postage	3

Sales for the month of February had amounted to £1,400,
which had all been paid into the bank account.

CAPITAL SECTION

Dr	Shop Premises Account	Cr	Dr	Motor Van Account	Cr
Barclays Bank A/c £3,250			Barclays Bank A/c £540		

	Shop Fittings Account			Purchase of Goods Account	
Barclays Bank A/c £1,200			Barclays Bank A/c £800		

Dr	K. McDonald—Capital Account	Cr
	Barclays Bank A/c £6,000	

Barclays Bank Account

Income of a *capital* nature	Capital A/c	£6,000	Shop Premises A/c	£3,250	Capital expenditure
			Shop Fittings A/c	1,200	
			Motor Van A/c	540	
			Purchase of Goods A/c	800	
			Balance c/d	210	
		£6,000		£6,000	
Income of a *revenue* nature	Balance b/d	£210	Light and Heat A/c	£5	Revenue expenditure
	Sales A/c	1,400	Insurance A/c	2	
			Wages A/c	40	
			Postage A/c	3	
			Purchase of Goods A/c	400	
			Balance c/d	1,160	
		£1,610		£1,610	
	Balance b/d	£1,160			

REVENUE SECTION

Dr	Light and Heat Account	Cr	Dr	Insurance Account	Cr
Barclays Bank A/c £5			Barclays Bank A/c £2		

	Wages Account			Postages Account	
Barclays Bank A/c £40			Barclays Bank A/c £3		

	Purchase of Goods Account			Sales Account	
Barclays Bank A/c £400				Barclays Bank A/c £1,400	

NOTE: Once again it is emphasised that goods purchased *during* a period of trading are regarded as coming under the "revenue section," *i.e.* such purchases are treated as items of *revenue* expenditure.

The value of the unsold stock (at cost price) on 28th February amounted to £100.

For the purpose of this example, the details of which have been set out opposite, all the items of *capital expenditure* which were needed to put the business into a position to commence trading have been placed in a box headed "capital section."

They have been shown in this manner to give emphasis to the expression "expenditure on capital account" or, as it is more commonly called, "capital expenditure." The intention is that the student shall see clearly that there is a world of difference between the owner's "Capital Account" and "*expenditure* on capital account."

The details of *trading* have all been included in the lower box headed "Revenue section." At the end of the period all of these details will be transferred to either the Trading Account or to the Profit and Loss Account.

THE REVENUE ACCOUNT

6. The purpose of the Revenue Account. It is appropriate, at this point, to introduce an expression which is commonly used in accounting circles. Sometimes one finds that a particular item of expenditure, because of its nature, might have to be split, part being debited to the Trading Account and part being charged to the Profit and Loss Account. This frequently happens in the case of *manufacturing* firms which, in addition to the normal Trading and Profit and Loss Accounts, have to prepare a "Manufacturing Account." Firms of this type have, therefore, to prepare *three* final accounts instead of the more usual two.

If we wished to indicate that a certain item of expenditure had to be split, some part of it being debited in either the Manufacturing Account or the Trading Account and the remainder in the Profit and Loss Account, it would be very cumbersome to have to indicate *by name* each of the accounts concerned. To overcome this difficulty the term "Revenue Account" is often used to cover the position without one being forced to be pedantically precise.

7. Distinguishing between capital and revenue expenditure. Even though the distinction between capital and revenue expenditure is, in theory at least, quite clear, it has been found that students do have difficulty in some cases in fully appreciating this distinction. It would appear that the difficulty arises mainly because they do not realise that *the maintenance* of an asset *in working order* is an expense of a *revenue* nature. For example, if they are asked how they would treat the cost of a set of new tyres fitted to a motor vehicle, many of them will say, "Capital expenditure," without a moment's hesitation although, in fact, it is always treated as revenue expenditure. They will argue, not without logic, that this is an "improvement" and one can see their point. Should they then be told that if a floor of cheap wood such as deal were replaced by an oak floor, and that this would be regarded by the Inspector of Taxes as an "improvement" of a *capital* nature, they become really confused. One can readily sympathise.

It is fortunate, however, that the explanation is quite simple. The important point on which attention must be focused is the *nature* of the asset. Motor vehicles and machinery have many moving parts which wear out in a comparatively short time. In order to maintain them as operationally safe and efficient units they must be kept in good repair. Their working life is usually limited to a few years only and as a result the *replacement* of parts is regarded as "revenue" expenditure. Such expense is normally charged under the heading "Repairs." These repairs may be split up into a number of accounts, *e.g.* Motor Repairs or Repairs to Office Machines.

On the other hand the replacement of a cheap floor by a highly expensive one should, strictly speaking, be capitalised. (In the context of accountancy, "to capitalise" means to convert money *received as income* into some permanent form of investment which will, in its turn, produce income in the future.) The reason for this is that such a floor may be expected to last perhaps for a hundred years. It can be seen, therefore, that the *nature* of the asset is a most important factor when deciding whether the expense is to be regarded as one of revenue or of capital.

The following table may be of assistance to students in helping them to reach a decision.

REVENUE EXPENDITURE	CAPITAL EXPENDITURE

Motor vehicles:
  Replacement of tyres
     ,,   ,, engine
     ,,   ,, parts
  General maintenance and overhauls.
	Motor vehicles:
	  Original cost of new or second-hand vehicles.

Machinery:
  Replacement of worn parts
  General maintenance.
	Machinery:
	  Original cost of new or second-hand machines.

Buildings:
  Periodical redecorations, *e.g.* interior painting and wall papering
  Roof and gutter repairs
  Replacing broken windows
  Electrical repairs
  External painting and repairs to brickwork, etc.
	Buildings:
	  Original cost of buildings
	  Cost of additions, *e.g.* extension to original building
	  Cost of expensive improvements.

Office equipment:
  Repairs to office machines
    ,,   ,,   ,, furniture.
	Office equipment:
	  Cost of original equipment either new or second-hand.

Shop fixtures and fittings:
  Repairs in general
  Cost of periodical servicing.
	Shop fixtures and fittings:
	  Cost of original items either new or second-hand.

NOTE: The above lists are not to be regarded as being complete and are only given as suggestions.

PROGRESS TEST 13

Theory

1. What are the two types of expenditure called? **(1)**
2. What is the reason for investing capital in the form of money in a business? **(2)**
3. Define (*a*) capital expenditure and (*b*) revenue expenditure. **(3, 4)**
4. Under which of the above heads of expense would you include the purchase of goods? **(5)**
5. What do you understand by the term "Revenue Account"? **(6)**
6. Make a list of items which fall under the heading of (*a*) capital expenditure and (*b*) revenue expenditure. **(7)**

Practice

7. Explain what you understand by:

(a) capital expenditure
(b) revenue expenditure.

8. What effect would the following transactions have on the balance sheet of a private trader?

(a) An increase in the stock of goods, through the purchase on credit from a supplier, totalling £200.
(b) A fire at the works which causes loss of machinery, not covered by insurance, £350.
(c) The purchase of machinery by cheque, £600.
(d) The failure of a Savings Bank in which the business has £1,000 invested.

9. A firm received an invoice from the Northern Gas Board containing the following details:

1. Gas consumed	£14·40
2. Hire of equipment	2·00
3. Repairs to installations	3·00
4. Quarterly H.P. instalment on gas-fired furnace	8·20
5. Large boiler coke	18·70
6. New gas fire	14·80
7. Annual maintenance charge (on installations)	3·50
	£64·60

Which of the above items would be regarded as capital expenditure and which as revenue expenditure? You are required to open whatever ledger accounts you consider necessary including an account for the Northern Gas Board in order to show the positions.

CHAPTER XIV

DEPRECIATION

THE DETERIORATION OF ASSETS

1. The meaning of "depreciation." This term is used in the accounting field to indicate *a loss of value*.

We apply the term to the assets of a business which lose value during the course of a period of trading. The reason for this loss of value may vary depending upon the nature of the particular asset. For example, a lease of factory premises is granted for a period of 20 years. Each year one-twentieth of the cost will be deducted from the price paid and *charged against* that particular year's profit, so at the end of twenty years the value of the lease will be reduced to nil. Again, a motor vehicle will lose its value as a result of use, and, in addition, because of the dating of the model (even though it might not be used at all).

While we normally consider depreciation to be an item which only affects assets of a fixed nature, such as machinery, building, furniture or motor cars, it must be realised that *some loss in value* (which is really what depreciation amounts to) may take place in other assets which are of a less permanent nature. Stocks of goods may easily lose their value in certain circumstances, *e.g.* a business dealing in ladies' gowns may suffer considerably if left with unsold dresses since these garments date very quickly. Stocks in any business could lose their value owing to a reduction in price which puts their current cost of replacement below their original cost. The method of dealing with losses in value of these "current," or "floating," assets differs from that used with fixed assets but it is referred to here to remind the student that a flexible approach must be used when considering depreciation.

In this study we are concerned only with the depreciation of *fixed* assets.

Fixed assets are purchased for the purpose of maintaining or increasing the profit-earning capacity and efficiency of a business in one way or another. Machinery is bought to increase productive capacity and thereby, it is hoped, to sell more and earn greater profits. New typewriters are purchased to aid the office staff in their work and to enable them to turn out a better looking finished product.

PROVIDING FOR DEPRECIATION

2. The element of time in the calculation of depreciation. We have already dealt with capital expenditure and revenue expenditure in the previous chapter. The student should, therefore, be quite clear as to the *difference* between these two types of expense and, what is equally important, the manner in which they are dealt with in accountancy.

We know that all businesses must incur *revenue* expenditure. This is another way of saying that the payment of wages, rent and many other expenses has to be made. In addition, every business must also incur *capital* expenditure in some form or another. Take, for example, a manufacturer of furniture who has to buy machinery which he estimates will last for, let us say, ten years. At the end of those ten years he expects that the machines will have to be replaced. Now, it is clear that the amount of money he pays out in wages and other revenue costs during those ten years, as well as the amount he has had to pay for the machinery, which was to last ten years, are both items of expense although of different types. But *they must both be paid for*. Looked at from the layman's point of view both (*a*) the wages paid and (*b*) the cost of the machinery are *costs of production*.

The difference between the two types of cost is that in the case of wages and general expenses the benefit is *immediate*, while in the case of the machinery the benefit is *spread over several trading periods*. Thus the fundamental difference is a difference of time only. Wages and general expenses are paid for as soon as the expense is incurred; the benefit is immediate and the payment is also immediate. On the other hand, the machinery is paid for before any benefit is obtained from it but the benefits are expected to last for a number of years. Without the machinery the business could not operate and so *each year* a certain charge for the use of the machinery is debited against the profits. This would obviously have to be done if the machinery were hired instead of being owned.

This charge, which is debited in the Revenue Account, is *the estimated loss of value* of the machinery during the year. When such action is taken it is spoken of as "writing off depreciation" or "making a provision for depreciation." The effect of this is to *reduce the profits* on the one hand and to *reduce the value of the asset* on the other.

EXAMPLE

A manufacturer pays £1,000 for a machine at the beginning of year No. 1 on, say, 1st January 19-1. Its life is expected to be five years. In addition, he pays wages of £800 each year and general expenses of £600 annually. He prepares his accounts at the end of each year.

Assuming that the machine is to be depreciated *by an equal amount* each year the profits will be reduced in year no. 1 by the following charges:

Wages		£800
General expenses		600
Depreciation of machinery:		
Cost of machine	£1,000	
Estimated life: 5 years		
Annual charge for depreciation:		
$\frac{1}{5} \times £1,000$		200
Total charges during year no. 1		£1,600

The Machinery Account would appear thus:

Machinery Account

19-1				19-1			
Jan. 1	Bank A/c		£1,000	Dec. 31	Depreciation A/c		£200
				31	Balance c/d		800
			£1,000				£1,000
19-2							
Jan. 1	Balance b/d		£800				

In this example the charges for wages and expenses every year are respectively £800 and £600. We have calculated the annual charge for depreciation at £200. Therefore the same total of £1,600 will be *the yearly charge* against the profits.

Each year until the end of year no. 5, *i.e.* 31st December 19-5, the same sums will be charged against the profits amounting, *in all*, to:

Wages	£4,000 (*i.e.* 5 × £800)
General expenses	3,000 (*i.e.* 5 × £600)
Depreciation of machinery	1,000 (*i.e.* 5 × £200)
	£8,000

If we now suppose that the business did not produce accounts each year but only once in *five* years then we would expect to find the charges for running the business exactly as set out above. That is to say, the *total cost* of the machinery would appear as a plain and simple charge against the profit of the (5-year) period. The Machinery Account would appear as follows:

Machinery Account

19-1			19-5		
			Dec. 31	Depreciation	
Jan. 1	Bank A/c	£1,000		A/c	£1,000

The fundamental difference in the treatment of capital expenditure and revenue expenditure is thus clearly seen to be a difference in *time* only.

3. Modern accounting treatment of depreciation. When dealing with the subject of depreciation there is one particular matter of some importance to be illustrated and emphasised. This is the question of modern accounting treatment which has become necessary as a result of the *Companies Act*, 1948. The Act lays down that limited companies must show in their balance sheets the *total amount of depreciation* which has been written off *since the fixed assets were acquired*. It thus becomes necessary for depreciation to be treated in a special manner so that this information may be readily forthcoming.

Instead of crediting annually any depreciation to the asset account concerned and thus showing *a reducing balance* on it (the asset account) this account is left untouched showing only *the original cost* of the item. An *additional account* is opened and is given the name "Provision for Depreciation Account" (or some similar heading) and each year the *annual* amount of depreciation is *credited* thereto. The corresponding *debit* entry will be made in a "Depreciation Account."

EXAMPLE

Office equipment costing £2,000 was purchased on 1st January 19-1, and £200 per annum is to be written off by way of depreciation.

Office Equipment Account

19-1			
Jan. 1	Bank A/c	£2,000	

At the end of the first year the following entries would be made:

Provision for Depreciation Account

	19-1		
	Dec. 31	Depreciation A/c	£200

Depreciation Account

19-1			
Dec. 31	Provision for Depreciation A/c	£200	

This account would then be closed off by a transfer to the Profit and Loss Account as follows:

Depreciation Account

19-1			19-1		
Dec. 31	Provision for Depreciation A/c	£200	Dec. 31	Transfer to Profit and Loss A/c	£200

Profit and Loss Account

Depreciation of Office Equipment £200	

Exactly the same procedure would be followed in each succeeding year. That is to say:

(*a*) *No entries* would be made in the *Office Equipment Account* after the first one recording the purchase of the equipment.

(*b*) £200 would be credited *each year* to the Provision for Depreciation Account.

(*c*) £200 would be debited each year to the Profit and Loss Account (via the Depreciation Account).

Therefore at the end of, say, three years the Office Equipment Account and the Provision for Depreciation Account would appear as shown below:

Office Equipment Account

19–1		
Jan. 1 Bank A/c	£2,000	

Provision for Depreciation Account

	19–1	
	Dec. 31 Depreciation A/c	£200
	19–2	
	Dec. 31 Depreciation A/c	200
	19–3	
	Dec. 31 Depreciation A/c	200
		————
		£600

TWO DIFFERENT WAYS OF CALCULATING DEPRECIATION

4. Methods of computing the charge for depreciation. Depreciation may be calculated in a number of different ways. In some cases the *type* of asset lends itself naturally to a particular method of depreciation, *e.g.* a lease granted for a definite number of years. In general, however, the following two methods are the ones most commonly employed since they can be applied to almost any kind of asset comparatively easily.

5. The "straight-line" or "fixed instalment" method. To operate this method it is necessary to know:

   (*a*) the *cost* of the asset;
   (*b*) its *number of years* of expected life;
   (*c*) the approximate *scrap-value* at the end of its life.

Having deducted the estimated scrap-value from the cost we divide the result by the number of years of the asset's *expected* life. This gives us the *fixed amount of depreciation* to be charged *every year* until the value of the asset has been reduced to nil.

Since all depreciation calculations must, by their very nature, be guesswork, this method is regarded as being the most suitable for general use, *the annual charge* against the profits *being constant.*

6. The "diminishing balance" or "reducing instalment" method. To operate this method *an arbitrary percentage* is chosen having regard to the expected length of working life of the asset. At the end of the first year this percentage is applied to the *original* cost of the asset and the amount so ascertained *deducted* therefrom. At the end of the second year *the same percentage* will be applied to the balance *as reduced* at the end of the first year. This pattern will be followed year after year. When this method is used the asset will *never* be reduced to nil. One factor which is regarded as rendering this method inequitable is that the amounts charged against profits in the early years will be *disproportionately greater* than those charged in the later years.

EXAMPLE

A machine which cost £12,000 had an expected life of 10 years. It was anticipated that it would have a scrap value of £2,000 at the end of that time.

FIXED INSTALMENT METHOD			REDUCING INSTALMENT METHOD		
Cost of asset		£12,000	Cost of asset		£12,000
Deduct: Estimated scrap value		2,000	Deduct: Estimated scrap value		2,000
		£10,000			£10,000
Less: Depreciation at 10% per annum			Less: Depreciation at 15% per annum		
Year 1	£1,000		Year 1	£1,500	
2	1,000		2	1,275	
3	1,000		3	1,083	
4	1,000		4	921	
5	1,000		5	783	
6	1,000		6	666	
7	1,000		7	566	
8	1,000		8	481	
9	1,000		9	409	
10	1,000		10	348	
		10,000			8,032
Book value at end of ten years		£ Nil	Balance at end of ten years not written off		£1,968

It is interesting to study and compare the two tables set out above. Points to note particularly are that with the reducing instalment method we have had to use an annual rate for depreciation of 15 per cent against the 10 per cent of the fixed instalment method; the amount of depreciation in the early years is very high and in the closing years quite low, i.e. £3,858 in the first three years as against £1,238 in the last three years; even then there still remains a balance of £1,968 at the end of the tenth year which, even if the anticipated £2,000 scrap value be realised, will still have to be written off against the profits of that year (assuming, of course, that the machine will be replaced this year).

There are other methods by which depreciation is calculated but at this early stage of study they will not be discussed.

PROGRESS TEST 14

Theory

1. Explain why it is necessary to make a charge in the Revenue Account for the depreciation of fixed assets. (1)

2. In what ways does the charge for depreciation differ from ordinary revenue expenditure? (2)

3. Describe how you would make a "provision" for depreciation. (3)

4. What is the object of operating a "Provision for Depreciation Account"? Why must limited companies, in particular, deal with depreciation in this manner? (3)

5. Describe the two principal ways in which depreciation may be calculated and state what basic information is required. (4, 5, 6)

Practice

6. A motor vehicle which cost £2,400 was bought on 1st January 19–2. Final accounts were prepared annually to 31st December and depreciation of vehicles is provided at 25 per cent p.a. by the diminishing balance method. Give the ledger entries in the Motor Vehicle Account for the first two years of the vehicle's working life assuming that the depreciation is to be written off the Vehicle Account, *i.e.* the asset account is not to be maintained at cost.

7. A machine was bought on credit for £3,000 on 1st April 19–2. The estimated working life of the machine is 7 years and the estimated scrap value is £200. The machine account is to be maintained *at cost*. Accounts are prepared annually to 30th September. Give the entries in the ledger accounts to record the machine and its depreciation up to 30th September, 19–4. Show how the machine would appear in the balance sheet at 30th September 19–4. (You are to use the "straight-line" method of depreciation.)

CHAPTER XV

PROVISIONS AND ACCRUED EXPENSES

THE LIABILITY FOR SERVICES RENDERED

1. The treatment of amounts owing for services. So far, when preparing the Profit and Loss Account at the end of the trading period we have only taken into consideration the amounts of money which have *actually been paid* for expenses during the course of that period. This is what we would expect since all the time we have been primarily concerned with transactions which have, in fact, been completed. We have *not* considered those expenses which we have had to incur but which remain *unpaid* at the end of the financial year. For example, if we employ staff we have to pay them. Pay day is usually on each Friday but the year end may fall on, say, a Wednesday, in which case there would be at least three days' wages owed *to* the employees, *i.e.* for Monday, Tuesday and Wednesday. We do not disturb our normal paying arrangements simply because the year end happens to fall on some day other than our usual pay day. Our staff must wait until pay day before drawing their wages. None the less, there can be no denying the fact that we have received *the benefit* of their work for those three days without paying them and as a result *a liability* has been incurred. If our accounts are to reflect the true position then we must take such matters into consideration.

There are, in fact, alternative ways in which the matter may be handled but we will use the most simple method because of its clarity. The other ways, while being technically correct, are less straightforward.

EXAMPLE

A business starts trading on 1st January 19-1. The bill for electricity for the three months ending 31st March 19-1 amounts to £21; it is received on 14th April and *paid* on 3rd May. For the second quarter the bill for £12 comes in on 16th July and is *paid* on 8th August. The bill for the third quarter of £9 reaches the firm on 15th October and is *settled* on 2nd November. The business year ends on 31st December and the charge for the last quarter's electricity is ascertained to be £25.

Payment of the quarterly accounts would have been made as follows:

Electricity Account

May 3	Bank A/c	£21		
Aug. 8	Bank A/c	12		
Nov. 2	Bank A/c	9		
		——		
		£42		

At 31st December 19-1, the end of the financial year, the sum of £25 *is owing*. This sum is, therefore, entered on *the debit side* of the account and then *carried down as a credit balance* as follows:

Electricity Account

19-1					
May 3	Bank A/c	£21			
Aug. 8	Bank A/c	12			——
Nov. 2	Bank A/c	9			
Dec. 31	**Balance c/d**	25			
		——			
		£67			≡≡
			19-2		
			Jan. 1	**Balance b/d**	£25

The credit balance of £25 is spoken of as being an "expense creditor." It can be seen that the credit side contains neither entries nor a total. This has been done deliberately so that the reader can see precisely how the account will finally be *closed*, *i.e.* by entering £67 *on the credit side*, this sum then being transferred to the *debit* of the Profit and Loss Account.

2. Entries in the Trial Balance. If the adjustment for the amount outstanding (*i.e.* unpaid) at the *end* of the period is entered in the account *before* the Trial Balance is extracted it will be necessary to make *two* entries therein. In the example given above we see that £67 has been entered on the debit side of the account. This consists of £42 which has *already* been paid plus £25 in respect of the expense incurred *during the last three months* which is still owing. In such a case the Trial Balance entries would read:

	Dr	Cr
Electricity	£67	
,, creditor		£25

NOTE: This will *only* apply if the adjustment is made in the ledger *before* taking out the Trial Balance. If no adjustment is made then only £42 will appear as a Trial Balance debit *no reference being made to the provision.*

3. The entries during the following year. When a balance representing an "expense creditor" is carried forward into the following period of trading the amount will normally be paid fairly early in that new period and will thus leave the account clear. Let us suppose that the balance of £25 was duly paid on 4th February 19-2. The account would appear thus (after payment had been made):

Electricity Account

19-2			19-2		
Feb. 4 Bank A/c		£25	Jan. 1 Balance b/d		£25

The account is thus clear for payments to be entered which will be made for electricity charges during 19-2.

ESTIMATES

4. Estimates and their effect. What is the effect of the use of estimates on the net profit both for this year and next year? When the estimate is made we should be in no doubt that the net profit must be wrong if the estimate is wrong. The amount of the error will, of course, be the difference between the estimate and the actual expense. To this extent, then, our profit will be affected. If the estimate of expense is too great our profit will be reduced; if, on the other hand, the estimate is too small our profit will be increased—on paper that is to say.

The effect on next year's accounts will be the opposite of the

ffect on this year's accounts. This simply means that taking
ne year's results with another errors in estimates cancel each
ther out.

PREPAYMENTS

5. Payments in advance. We have seen how provisions for
ccrued expenses should be dealt with in the preceding sections
nd now we must look at the other side of the picture, *i.e.* when
1ore money has been spent than should be charged against the
rofit of a particular trading period.

It stands to reason that if a business spends more than is
rictly chargeable against the profits of a particular trading
eriod an adjustment should be made to ensure that *the correct
mount of expense* is debited in the Profit and Loss Account. It
1ust be understood that sometimes the only way that a
usiness can obtain some vital service such as insurance is by
aying for a whole year *in advance*. As a general rule the in-
urance company will not do business on any other terms!
'ery often it becomes necessary for a particular form of in-
urance cover to be obtained at a particular date during a
rading period. Since the insurance companies will only do
usiness on their own terms (and these terms normally require
hat insurance premiums must be paid for on a basis of twelve
1onths from the date of the start of the insurance cover) we
vill sometimes have to pay a premium (as the annual cost of
1surance is called) which runs well into next year's trading
eriod.

EXAMPLE

A business has its year end at 31st December. On 1st May
19–1 it bought a motor van and insured it for the following
twelve months. The premium paid was £36.

We can see that the monthly cost of the insurance is £3 and
that there are eight months from 1st May to 31st December.
This means that £24 worth of insurance *will have been used up* at
the end of the financial year of the business. This figure of £24
is, therefore, the proper amount which has to be charged against
the profits. At the moment, however, £36 is the sum which has
been entered in the books. We must, therefore, consider that the
difference of £12 is a *debt* which is *owed to* the business by the

insurance company. Accordingly, we will have to take steps to record this in the books, as follows:

Insurance Account

19-1			19-1		
May 1	Bank A/c	£36	Dec. 31	Profit and Loss A/c	£2

Even though the figure of £12 is, strictly speaking, a deb *owing to the business* from the insurance company we keep th book-keeping as simple as possible and do not normally open a account for the insurance company showing it as a debtor. W obtain precisely the same effective result by entering *the unuse amount* on the credit side of the Insurance Account and carryin it down *as a debit balance* in the following manner:

Insurance Account

19-1			19-1		
May 1	Bank A/c	£36	Dec. 31	Profit and Loss A/c	£2
			31	Balance c/d	1
		£36			£3
19-2					
Jan. 1	Balance b/d	£12			

6. Deferred revenue expenditure. This rather imposing titl refers to revenue expenditure which *has been paid* during on accounting period but part of which will apply to one or mor *future* accounting periods. It is another way of expressin payments in advance.

The term "deferred revenue expenditure" is more usuall applied, however, to certain special cases such as experimenta work or the costs of development of a new process. The reaso for the expense to be treated in this way is that it is so heav that it would be unfair to charge it entirely to the period durin which it was incurred since the benefits resulting will be fel over a long period in the future. The expenditure is, therefore spread over what may be termed "the period of benefit."

PROVISIONS AND RESERVES

7. Different kinds of provisions. We have already seen in Chapter XIV that a *provision* for depreciation is entered as a *charge* against the profits of a trading period. As a result the profit for that period is reduced.

Earlier in this chapter we learned how "provisions" can be made for *accrued* expenditure by debiting expenses that have been *incurred* but for which no payment has been made at the date of the balance sheet. The *effect* of making any such provisions is to *reduce* the profit. Thus a provision may be for any of the following things:

(*a*) depreciation of an asset,

(*b*) to anticipate bad debts;

(*c*) in respect of an expense which has been incurred but has not yet been paid.

8. Reserves. Reserves can only come into existence after the net profit has been ascertained. Normally, they are created by limited companies but occasionally one meets with them elsewhere. The idea of creating a reserve is to *set aside* a part of the profit, *i.e. leaving it in the business* instead of the owner (or owners) drawing it out and using it privately. The object is to strengthen the financial position of the business by the prevention of its funds being drained away.

A reserve may be brought into being for a *specific* purpose, such as building up a fund for the renewal of a lease, but more often the reserve is for *general* purposes of the business. Where the reserve is for some specific purpose requiring money to be available at some future date money may be spent in buying assets such as Government Stocks for redemption when the due time comes.

This matter of setting aside profits to reserve is dealt with more fully in the author's book *Company Accounts* in the HANDBOOK series.

PROGRESS TEST 15

Theory

1. Describe a simple way of making a provision for an accrued expense. (1)

2. How is the liability for accrued expenses shown in the trial balance? (2)

3. Sometimes it is necessary to make estimates in respect of accrued expenses. What would be the effect of a wrong estimate, (a) on the current year's accounts and (b) on the following year's accounts? (4)

4. What is meant by the expression "prepayment"? If a prepayment is dealt with correctly when the final accounts are being prepared does this increase or reduce the profit? (5)

5. Explain what is meant by "deferred revenue expenditure." (6)

Practical

6. The following trial balance was extracted from the books of A. Christie on 31st December 19–1:

Capital		£30,000
Freehold premises	£20,000	
Fixtures and fittings	4,500	
Stock 1st January 19–1	4,864	
Purchases and sales	11,623	16,472
Returns inwards and outwards	119	133
Debtors and creditors	2,120	1,496
Drawings	1,500	
Staff salaries & commission	830	
Lighting and heating	115	
Rent, rates and insurance	260	
Sundry expenses	108	
Discounts allowed & received	22	124
Cash at bank	2,164	
	£48,225	£48,225

Prepare Trading and Profit and Loss Accounts for the year ended 31st December 19–1 and a balance sheet as at that date.

The following items must be brought into account at 31st December 19–1:

(a) 5% depreciation to be allowed on fixtures and fittings.
(b) Rates paid in advance, £25.
(c) Commission due but unpaid, £20.
(d) Stock on hand at 31st December 19–1 was valued at £4,762.

7. The following trial balance was extracted from the books of F. Hill, a retailer, at 31st December 19–2:

Capital		£2,700
Drawings	£680	
Fixtures and fittings	950	
Delivery van	250	

Sales		3,870
Purchases	2,610	
Discount received		115
Wages	245	
Rent and rates	210	
Insurance	27	
Stock at 1st January 19–2	820	
Sundry creditors		257
Sundry debtors	253	
Cash at bank	871	
Cash in hand	26	
	£6,942	£6,942

Prepare Trading and Profit and Loss Account for the year ended 31st December 19–2 and a balance sheet at that date, taking into account the following:

At 31st December 19–2:

Stock	£850
Accrued rent	15
Insurance unexpired	9
Rates in advance	12

Depreciation is to be provided on the van at 20 per cent p.a. and on fixtures and fittings at 10 per cent p.a.

Give the percentage of gross profit to sales.

8. The following points were discovered in the books of a contractor before the closing entries had been made. Final accounts had been prepared in draft form and showed a net profit of £4,027.

(a) The purchase of a new cement mixer for £150 was included in Motor Expenses Account.

(b) The proprietor's Drawings Account included two items, each of £50, being the road fund tax in respect of (a) a van used by the business and (b) his own private car.

(c) £30 paid by a customer, K. Kingsley, had been credited to K. Kinsey's account in error.

(d) The rates on the proprietor's private house, £142, had been paid by the business and debited to Rates Account.

(e) £126 included in Wages Account was paid to workmen for building a garage at the proprietor's private house.

(f) Materials bought on credit for £89 had been delivered to the business on the balance sheet date and included in the stock figure at that date, but the invoice for these goods had not been entered in the purchase day book.

You are required to prepare a statement showing the effect of these adjustments on the profit previously ascertained in the draft accounts.

CHAPTER XVI

BAD AND DOUBTFUL DEBTS

BAD DEBTS

1. The treatment of bad debts. Sometimes a business sells goods to a customer who, later on, finds himself in financial difficulties of such magnitude that he is unable to pay off his debt. Such a debt, which it is now impossible to collect, is called a "*bad* debt." In such circumstances there is only one course of action open to the firm which is owed the money. This is to "write off the debt," *i.e.* to cancel it.

When goods are sold on credit the seller obviously sells in the full expectation that the customer will, in due time, pay for the goods. If the seller had any doubts about the integrity of his customer or of his ability to pay, common sense tells us that he would take care to ensure in some way or another that he, the seller, *would not suffer a loss*. He might insist on an *immediate* settlement for cash; he might refuse to part with the goods, or he might take precautions to see that settlement was made in a much shorter period of credit than is usually allowed. None the less, no matter what precautions businessmen take it is almost inevitable that at some time or another they will suffer a loss by incurring bad debts. Should this happen the account of the debtor will be credited (since this is the only way of clearing the balance on the account) and a corresponding debit will be made in a "Bad Debts Account." At the end of the trading period this account will be closed by making a transfer to the debit of Profit and Loss Account.

EXAMPLE

Snodgrass & Co. sold goods to the value of £60 to A. Welcher on 15th January. Welcher was adjudicated bankrupt on 23rd July and was unable to pay anything to his creditors. On 11th August, Snodgrass & Co. wrote off the debt and this was ultimately transferred to the Profit and Loss Account at 31st December. The entries would be as follows:

A. Welcher Account

Jan. 15	Sales A/c	£60

When Snodgrass & Co. were notified that the entire debt was to be regarded as bad it was written off.

A. Welcher Account

Jan. 15	Sales A/c	£60	Aug. 11	**Bad Debts A/c**	£60

Bad Debts Account

Aug. 11	**A. Welcher A/c**	£60

Thus what was once a debt due to the business, *i.e. an asset*, has now to be regarded as *an expense* which will, at the end of the financial year, *reduce the profit* by £60.

Bad Debts Account

			Dec. 31	**Profit and Loss A/c**	£60
Aug. 11	Bad Debts A/c	£60			

Profit and Loss Account

Dec. 31	**Bad Debts A/c**	£60

2. Bad debts recovered. Occasionally, we find that a debt which has been written off as bad is recovered at a later date, *i.e.* the debtor re-establishes himself financially and pays up either fully or in part.

Should this happy state of affairs come to pass the double entry to record the recovery should be as follows:

> *Dr* Cash Account or Bank Account;
> *Cr* The debtor's personal account.

This treatment is emphasised since textbooks in general state that the credit entry should be made in the Bad Debts Account. It must be stressed that, as a matter of business ethics any recovery of a bad debt should *first* be shown as a credit in the debtor's personal account. It is only fair that this should be done, for at some future date the debtor's account may be referred to for some reason. If from a scrutiny of the account he appears to be a *bad debtor, i.e.* one who failed and whose debt was written off, the obvious conclusion that the observer would draw is that the customer is not to be granted any future credit. On the other hand, if the recovery is shown the debtor does, in fact, get credit for his subsequent efforts to make good.

EXAMPLE

On 26th May in the following year Welcher, who had in the meantime inherited a large sum of money, sent a cheque for £60 to Snodgrass & Co. The entries would be in the first place a debit of £60 in the Bank Account, *Welcher's Account being credited.* The record of the recovery would then be shown as below:

A. Welcher Account

May 26	**Bad Debts A/c**	£60	May 26	Bank A/c	£60

Bad Debts Recovered Account

		May 26	**A. Welcher A/c** (bad debts previously written off now received in full) £60

At the end of the year the Bad Debts Recovered Account would be closed by a transfer of £60 *to the credit* of the Profit and Loss Account.

PROVISIONS FOR DOUBTFUL DEBTS

3. The meaning of the term "doubtful debts." A bad debt arises when, for any reason, a customer is *unable to pay* the amount he owes to his creditor. "Doubtful debts" are, as the name suggests, those debts whose collection is regarded as *uncertain, i.e.* they *may* finally become bad or they *may* be paid in full.

4. Making a provision for a specific debt. Sometimes the management of a business will become aware that a certain customer who owes it money is in difficult financial circumstances and that there is a distinct possibility of the debt now due becoming a bad debt at some future date. There is, however, at the present time no *certainty* of this happening. In such a case the prudent course for the business to take is to regard the debt as *doubtful*.

By this we mean that it is not enough simply to bear the facts in mind; *positive action should be taken*. We will suppose, initially, that the amount involved is a debt for £100. Clearly we have had to buy the goods in the first place at a cost price of, say, £80. We added 25 per cent as our profit mark-up thus giving a selling price of £100. It follows, therefore, that when we sell the goods *two elements* are present in the selling price: the element of cost, £80, and the element of profit, £20. Should our debtor fail to meet his obligations we stand to lose two things, (*a*) the amount we originally had to pay for the goods and (*b*) the profit which we have credited to our Profit and Loss Account.

Looking at a Trading and Profit and Loss Account consisting only of these goods we would see the position as follows:

Cost of goods	£80	Sales	£100
Gross profit c/d	20		
	——		——
	£100		£100
		Gross profit b/d	£20

We can see a profit of £20 standing to our credit but there is *a potential debit* of £100, which would obviously turn our profit of £20 into a loss of £80.

Now if this is indeed the position in which we find ourselves we would be most unwise to consider that we have made a profit of £20. Prudent counsels should prevail and force us to acknowledge that we may be faced *with a loss* of £80. This being so, what is the positive action which we should take?

The first step is to be completely pessimistic and *debit the full amount* of the debt, *i.e.* £100, to the Profit and Loss Account. That is to say, we treat the debt as though it were bad in so far as our calculation of profit for the period is concerned. *The corresponding credit* will be made in a new account called "Provision for Doubtful Debts Account." *No entry* is made in the debtor's personal account at this point.

The profit has now been *reduced* by £100. This will affect the Capital Account when the final transfer is made from the Profit and Loss Account, culminating in a reduction of the ultimate credit balance on that account. This, in turn, will *reduce the liabilities total* on the balance sheet.

What happens to the assets total? We can now look upon the *total* of the debtors balances as they appear in the ledger as not representing the true position, since this sum includes an item of £100 regarded as *doubtful*. We have, however, a credit balance on the "Provision for Doubtful Debts Account" which we can use to reduce the total of the debtors balances. Consequently, on the balance sheet we set out the debtors position as follows (assuming that the total of the debtors amounted to, say, £1,800):

Sundry debtors	£1,800	
Less Provision for doubtful debts	100	
		£1,700

As a result of this treatment the *total* of the "Assets" side of the balance sheet will be reduced by £100 and so conform with the reduction of £100 on the Liabilities side.

5. Making a "general" provision for doubtful debts. Some businesses find that it is prudent for them to make a general provision for doubtful debts at the end of each financial year. Experience has taught them that there is every likelihood that some of their customers will fail to pay their debts. Who these failures will be they cannot tell at this point but they know that almost certainly *some* will prove to be bad. The experience of years has shown them that, barring miracles, they will not collect all the money that is owing to them.

It follows, therefore, that some general provision ought to be made, *i.e.* the Profit and Loss Account will be *debited* with the amount of the provision considered necessary and "Provision for Doubtful Debts Account" credited in exactly the same way as was shown for making a provision for *a specific debt* which was regarded as doubtful. So, to show the exact position:

Dr Profit and Loss Account
Cr Provision for Doubtful Debts Account

It must be noted that when action is taken to make this general provision, the normal basis of calculation (gained by years of experience) is to make the amount of the provision *a percentage* of the actual total of the debts owing at the date of the balance sheet. For example, suppose that 3 per cent were the figure that the firm felt to be prudent and that the debtors amounted to £10,000 in total at the balance sheet date, then the provision would be 3 per cent of £10,000, *i.e.* £300. Therefore:

Dr	Profit and Loss Account	£300;
Cr	Provision for Doubtful Debts Account	£300.

INCREASING AND DECREASING THE PROVISIONS

6. Increasing the provision for doubtful debts. Since it is most unlikely that at the end of next year the debtors will, in total, amount to £10,000, some *adjustment* of the provision will have to be made. Remember that the provision is usually *a fixed percentage* of the *total debtors* at the end of each year.

There are two alternative methods of dealing with last year's provision.

Method 1. In this case a separate Bad Debts Account is operated for those debts which *actually prove to be bad* during the year (and which are written off). The Provision for Doubtful Debts Account remains *isolated*. It therefore follows that should *any debts* become bad during the year they will be written off to the Bad Debts Account, *i.e.* the customer's personal account is credited and the Bad Debts Account debited. It should be pointed out here that the words "any debts" used above mean (*a*) any debts which were owing *at the start* of the first day's trading in that financial year or (*b*) any debts which were contracted *during the year* as a result of sales.

No entry will be made in the Provision for Doubtful Debts Account for these debts when they are written off.

EXAMPLE

At 31st December 19-1, a provision of £300 was made in respect of doubtful debts. Debtors amounted to £10,000. Included in this £10,000 was £137 owing by Adams. This was written off as bad on 27th June 19-2.

During the year 19-2 the following debtors proved to be bad: Blankson £43, for goods sold to him on 6th February 19-2 and

Charteris £162, for goods sold to him on 1st April 19-2. Blankson's debt was written off on 16th September 19-2, and that of Charteris on 4th November 19-2. At 31st December 19-2, the debtors amounted to £12,000 and Provision for Doubtful Debts Account was adjusted to an amount equal to 3 per cent of the total debtors, *i.e.* a provision of £360.

The accounts in the books of the firm would appear as follows:

Adams

19-2			19-2		
			June 27	Transfer to **Bad Debts** A/c	£137
Jan. 1	Balance b/d	£137			

Blankson

19-2			19-2		
			Sept. 16	Transfer to **Bad Debts** A/c	£43
Feb. 6	Sales Day Book	£43			

Charteris

19-2			19-2		
			Nov. 4	Transfer to **Bad Debts** A/c	£162
Apr. 1	Sales day book	£162			

Bad Debts Account

19-2					
June 27	**Adams**	£137			
Sept. 16	**Blankson**	43			
Nov. 4	**Charteris**	162			

Provision for Doubtful Debts Account

			19-2		
			Jan. 1	Balance b/d	£300

It is most important that *the dates* of the entries in the above accounts be studied. The items have been shown in heavy type to assist in following the sequence.

We see that the three personal accounts have been ruled off thus indicating that no further entries will be made thereon. We are left with the two accounts dealing respectively with bad debts and doubtful debts. What action is to be taken at the end of the financial year, *i.e.* 31st December 19-2?

Let us deal, first of all, with the Bad Debts Account.

Bad Debts Account

19-2			19-2		
June 27	Adams	£137	Dec. 31	Transfer to	
Sept. 16	Blankson	43		Profit and	
Nov. 4	Charteris	162		Loss A/c	£342
		———			———
		£342			£342

Profit and Loss Account

19-2		
Dec. 31	Bad Debts A/c	£342

The outstanding matter remaining is to calculate *the new provision* which we are told is to be 3 per cent of the total debtors at 31st December 19-2. The debtors amount to £12,000 and the provision therefore is to be £360.

If we refer to the Provision Account we see that this stands at £300 *in credit*.

Last year the owner of the business deliberately *reduced* his profit when he made the provision of £300 by debiting Profit and Loss Account and crediting Provision for Doubtful Debts Account. That credit, as we can see, is still standing in the books.

The action now to be taken *to raise the existing provision* to £360 could hardly be more simple. The difference between £300 and £360 is £60. We therefore *debit* Profit and Loss Account and *credit* Provision for Doubtful Debts Account with £60, thus:

Profit and Loss Account

19-2		
Dec. 31	Bad Debts A/c	£342
Dec. 31	**Provision for Doubtful Debts A/c**	60

Provision for Doubtful Debts Account

19-2				19-2			
Dec. 31	Balance c/d	£360		Jan. 1	Balance b/d		£300
				Dec. 31	Profit and Loss A/c		60
		£360					£360
				19-3			
				Jan. 1	Balance b/d		£360

Examination of the Profit and Loss Account makes it perfectly clear that the profits of the business for the year 1972 are suffering total charges of £402 in respect of bad and doubtful debts, *i.e.* £342 in respect of *bad debts* which have been completely *written off* and £60 for *the increase in the provision* for doubtful debts.

Method 2. If the alternative method is used no Provision Account is employed. *All* items in respect of bad debts and doubtful debts are dealt with *in one account*, the "Bad Debts Account." The transactions set out above would be recorded in the following manner:

Bad and Doubtful Debts Account

19-2				19-2		
June 27	Adams	£137		Jan. 1	Balance b/d	£300
Sept. 16	Blankson	43		Dec. 31	Profit and Loss A/c	402
Nov. 4	Charteris	162				
Dec. 31	Balance c/d	360				
		£702				£702
				19-3		
				Jan. 1	Balance b/d	£360

The *final* figure debited to Profit and Loss Account is still £402, but in this case it is transferred *in one sum* instead of two.

It is quite obvious that the second method is much simpler in operation, but the first method has been explained in detail since a clear knowledge of the processes is demanded for examination work. In practice either method is equally acceptable.

7. Decreasing the provision for doubtful debts. Problems dealing with provisions for doubtful debts usually state that the provision is to be a certain percentage of the total debtors *at the date of the balance sheet* each year. Now the volume of the debts owing to a business can vary quite considerably from day to day or from week to week. We may therefore expect some variation between one year's end and another. This being so, if the *percentage* adopted by any particular firm remains unchanged the provision should be *relative* to the total of the unpaid debts. If, for instance, it were customary to make a provision of 5 per cent of the debts at the end of any year and the debtors were £7,000 one year and £3,000 the next, it would be incorrect to retain a provision of £350 (5% × £7,000) when it should be based on £3,000, *i.e.* £150.

EXAMPLE

H. Anderson decided to make a general provision for doubtful debts at 31st December 19-1. At that date he was owed £2,400 and he felt that a provision of 4 per cent would be adequate, *i.e.* £96.

Every debtor did, in fact, duly pay to Anderson the amount he owed during 19-2. Anderson still felt, however, that it was a good idea to maintain the Provision Account and he continued to do so. At 31st December 19-2 the debtors total amounted to £1,825 and, as in 19-1, he based his provision at 4 per cent of the total sum owing.

Using the Profit and Loss Account as an account of *original entry*, the *initial* provision at the end of 19-1 would have appeared as follows:

Profit and Loss Account for year ended 31st December 19-1

Provision for Doubtful Debts £96	

Provision for Doubtful Debts Account

19-1			19-1		
Dec. 31	Balance c/d	£96	Dec. 31	**Profit and Loss A/c**	£96
			19-2		
			Jan. 1	Balance b/d	£96

A year later the credit balance of £96 was *still* standing on the Provision Account. The total debtors had diminished to £1,825 but Anderson still wished to maintain the provision *relatively*, *i.e.* it was to be calculated, as before, at 4 per cent of *the total debtors*. These, however, had dropped to £1,825 as against £2,400 a year ago. 4 per cent of £1,825 amounts to £73 and this is the sum which will be *deducted* from the total of the debtors as they appear in the balance sheet.

It should be appreciated that the credit balance of £96 represents a deduction from the *19–1* profits and that this sum of £96 *has not been touched* during 19–2. As has been shown the provision required for 19–2 is £73 which is *less* than the *existing* provision. All we need to do in such a case is to subtract £73 from £96, *i.e.* £23, *debiting* the Provision Account and *crediting* the *19–2* Profit and Loss Account with this sum. The balance remaining on the Provision Account, £73, is then carried forward into 19–3.

Provision for Doubtful Debts Account

19–2			19–2		
Dec. 31	**Profit and Loss** A/c	£23	Jan. 1	Balance b/d	£96
31	Balance c/d	73			
		£96			£96
			19–3		
			Jan. 1	Balance b/d	73

Profit and Loss Account for Year ended 31st December 19–2

	Provision for Doubtful Debts (*reduction* of existing provision) £23

PROGRESS TEST 16

Theory

1. What do you understand by the term "bad debt"? **(1)**
2. How is a bad debt "written off"? **(1)**
3. What entries are needed to record the recovery of a bad debt which had previously been written off? **(2)**
4. What is a "doubtful" debt? **(3)**

5. Provisions for doubtful debts may be either "specific" or "general." Explain these terms. **(4, 5)**

6. Show how you would set out debtors and any provisions for doubtful debts in a balance sheet. **(4)**

7. There are two methods of dealing with bad debts and the provision or doubtful debts. Explain the operation of these two methods. **(6)**

Practice

8. Parsons and Co. prepared accounts at the end of the first year of trading, showing a profit of £2,873. The firm was owed £1,780 at that time and it was decided that a provision for doubtful debts ought to be made. A provision amounting to 5 per cent of £1,780 was thought to be sufficient.

Make the entries in the books showing (*a*) the adjusted profit, (*b*) the entries in the Provision for Doubtful Debts Account and (*c*) how the debtors would be shown in the balance sheet.

9. G. Hardy commenced business on 1st April 19-2. When preparing his accounts at the end of the first year's trading he noted that bad debts written off during the year amounted to £260. He decided that it would be advisable to create a provision for doubtful debts at 31st March 19-3, in the sum of £450, which was 5 per cent of the debtors balances outstanding at that date.

During the year ended 31st March 19-4 debts amounting to £420 proved to be bad and were written off. £60 was recovered in respect of debts written off during the first year of trading. At 31st March 19-4, the outstanding debtors balances amounted to £16,000 and it was decided to continue to base the provision for doubtful debts on 5 per cent of the total debtors.

Set out the entries necessary to record the above matters in the ledger and show the total debit to Profit and Loss Account for the year ended 31st March 19-4 in respect of bad debts and provisions. (The student is reminded that he must use the Profit and Loss Account as an account of *original* entry.)

CHAPTER XVII

PROVISIONS FOR DISCOUNTS

DISCOUNTS ALLOWED

1. Introduction. We saw in Chapter XVI how prudence in financial matters is exercised when a special provision is made in respect of debts of a doubtful nature. We will now examine another aspect of "provisions" although the subject matter of what follows is perhaps of more academic than practical importance. However, since it *is* a little unusual this matter becomes a likely "examination point" and so the principles should be mastered.

2. Making a provision for discount allowed. We have already seen that when goods are sold on credit it is the custom in many trades for a small discount to be allowed for prompt payment, *i.e.* payment within an agreed time limit. Since the ability of a debtor to pay his debt within a certain time limit is something which is beyond the knowledge of the seller of the goods, the latter can never be sure whether or not he will be called upon to allow the discount, *i.e.* to accept less than the amount of the debt.

EXAMPLE

Snodgrass sells goods for £50 to Cleghorn on 11th August 19–1 and arranges that if Cleghorn pays by not later than 15th September he, Cleghorn, may take £2 discount. Snodgrass's trading year ends on 31st August.

This means that the amount of money which Snodgrass will receive in settlement of his debt will depend upon circumstances *entirely beyond his control*. If Cleghorn pays by 15th September he will deduct £2 from his debt of £50 and Snodgrass will only receive £48 *in full settlement* for a sale of £50.

Since the full amount of £50 will have been credited to Sales Account it will, in turn, be posted to the credit of Trading Account at 31st August and the proper amount of gross profit will be calculated on this item (along with all the other sales). The gross profit will then be brought down to the credit side of

Profit and Loss Account. Let us suppose that the amount of gross profit involved in this sale is £10, which would mean that the goods had cost £40.

Preparing a Trading Account in respect of this item alone we would have the following position:

Trading Account for year ended 31st August 19-1

Purchase of goods	£40	Sales		£50
Gross profit c/d	10			
	£50			£50

The Profit and Loss Account would then show:

	Gross profit b/d	£10

Assuming that there are no other expenses we can see clearly how dependent Snodgrass's *net profit* will be upon Cleghorn's decision as to the date when he will pay his debt, for if he does so by 15th September, Snodgrass will have to suffer a loss of £2 of gross profit in the form of "discount allowed" which will, of course, make his net profit £8 instead of the £10 he would otherwise have earned.

Now it has been emphasised that Snodgrass cannot know *in advance* whether Cleghorn will or will not take advantage of the discount arrangement. Since Snodgrass reaches the end of his trading year at 31st August he is left in a state of uncertainty with regard to Cleghorn's line of action in the matter. As a matter of plain financial prudence Snodgrass may well decide that he should be pessimistic and *anticipate* that Cleghorn will, in fact, pay within the time limit and thus cause him (Snodgrass) a loss of part of his gross profit. The action he should then take would be to open an account headed "Provision for Discounts Allowed" and credit this account with £2 making a corresponding debit entry in his Profit and Loss Account at 31st August.

The final position would therefore be:

Provision for Discounts Allowed Account

19-1			19-1		
Aug. 31	Balance c/d	£2	Aug. 31	**Profit and Loss A/c**	£2
			Sept. 1	Balance b/d	£2

Profit and Loss Account

Provision for Discounts Allowed A/c	£2	Gross profit	£10
Net Profit	8		
	£10		£10

3. Treatment in the balance sheet. The credit balance on the Provision for Discounts Allowed Account will be *deducted* from the total of the debtors which appears in the balance sheet in precisely the same way as a provision for bad or doubtful debts would be shown as a deduction. The situation in respect of the above example would be set out in the balance sheet thus:

Debtor	£50	
Less: Provision for Discounts Allowed	2	
		£48

4. An alternative method. Quite frequently we find examination questions specifically requiring us to make a "provision" in the Discount Account itself and not in a special Provision for Discount Allowed Account. Provided that the principle involved has been understood this alternative method should present no difficulty.

Taking the particulars of the above example, let us first of all imagine that it is the first time that a "provision" has ever been made for discounts. The Discounts Allowed Account would appear as follows:

Discount Allowed Account

19-1			19-1		
			Aug. 31 Profit and Loss		
Aug. 31 Balance c/d	£2		A/c	£2
			Sept. 1 Balance b/d	2

Profit and Loss Account ended 31st August 19-1

| Discount allowed | £2 | |

Comparison with the first method reveals a difference only in *the name* of the account. Let us now go a step further and deal with the position at *31st August 19-2, i.e.* one year later.

Suppose that the *total* of discounts allowed to customers during the trading year amounted to £87 and that the "provision" to be made at 31st August 19-2 was to be £3.

In the first place *the credit balance* of £2 on the Discount Allowed Account will have been "used up," so to speak, when the total of discounts for the year which have been allowed to customers (£87) is set against it. Secondly, a *new* provision of £3 must be provided. That is to say, it is anticipated that there may well be this *further* expense to be charged against the year's profits. The Discount Allowed Account would now appear as follows:

Discount Allowed Account

19-2				19-1			
Aug. 31	Sundry discounts allowed		£87	Sept. 1	Balance b/d		£2
31	Balance c/d (being *new* provision)		3	19-2 Aug. 31	**Profit and Loss A/c**		88
			———				———
			£90				£90
				19-2 Sept. 1	Balance b/d		£3

Profit and Loss Account year ended 31st August 19-2

Discount Allowed A/c	£88	

If the first method were used we would show the position at 31st August 19-2 as follows:

Provision for Discount Allowed Account

19-2				19-1			
Aug. 31	Balance c/d (being *new* provision)		£3	Sept. 1	Balance b/d		£2
				19-2 Aug. 31	Profit and Loss A/c		1
			———				———
			£3				£3
				19-2 Sept. 1	Balance b/d		£3

Discount Allowed Account

19-2			19-2		
Aug. 31	Sundry discounts allowed	£87	Aug. 31	Profit and Loss A/c	£87

Profit and Loss Account for year ended 31st August 19-2

Provision for discount allowed	£1
Discount allowed	87
	£88

From all this we can see that the effect upon the profit is precisely the same whichever method is used. We can also see that just as the *making of a provision* in respect of bad or doubtful debts reduces the profit (by being debited in the Profit and Loss Account) so too does the *making of a provision* for discounts allowed.

> NOTE: In examination problems you must remember that if a *provision for discounts* is required *as well as* a provision for "Bad and doubtful debts" you must always deduct the "Bad and doubtful debts provision" from the Debtors *before* dealing with the provision for Discounts.
>
> The reason is simple. If a debt is bad you will not get any of your money. Therefore when you make the provision for bad and doubtful debts you are saying, in effect, "I do not expect that I will ever receive any of this money." In other words, you are saying that you do not count the amount as being owed to you.
>
> It follows, therefore, that if you are not going to treat the item as a debt owing to you, you cannot logically make a provision in respect of any discount you may have to allow your debtor.
>
> Since you have already *written off* the entire debt, the matter ends there.

PROVISIONS FOR DISCOUNTS RECEIVED

5. A deduction from the creditors. In practice, it is very rare to find firms making a provision for discounts which they propose to take at a future date since prudence strongly discourages profits of a doubtful nature from being credited *before* they have been realised. Since examiners sometimes require the point to be answered, however, an example is given below.

EXAMPLE

A provision for discounts receivable amounting to £60 is to be made in a firm's accounts for the year ended 31st December 19–2.

In this case *profit is being anticipated* and the Profit and Loss Account must, therefore, be credited with £60—the corresponding debit being entered in the Provision for Discounts Received Account. As a result of this *anticipation* of profit the liability appearing in the Balance Sheet in the form of the total sum owed to creditors will have to be *reduced* by a similar amount. The Capital Account of the owner will, on the other hand, be credited with this additional amount of profit and this will have the effect of increasing the total of the liabilities side by £60. There will thus be no change in the total of the liabilities side.

PROGRESS TEST 17

Theory

1. Explain the reasoning behind a trader's decision to make a provision for discount to be allowed to a customer. (2)
2. How should a "Provision for discounts to be allowed" be shown in the balance sheet? (3)
3. When making a provision for discounts to be allowed as well as making a provision for doubtful debts, which of these provisions should be calculated first? (4)
4. Is it a good principle to create a provision for discounts received? (5)

Practice

5. The trial balance of a business as at 31st December showed, among other items in the debit column, the following:

> Provision for discount on creditors
> (at 1st January previous)   £390

You learned that the provision required for the discount on creditors at 31st December was to be adjusted to 2½ per cent of the amount owing to trade creditors at that date. Creditors were owed £21,600.

Make the adjustment you consider necessary to amend the Provision for Discounts Receivable Account to conform with the above requirement.

6. From the following trial balance and notes relating to a retail business you are required to prepare a Trading and Profit and Loss Account for the year ended 31st May 1971 and a balance sheet as at that date. Give careful attention to layout and presentation.
At 31st May 19-1:

(a) the stock was valued at £3,100,
(b) salaries due but unpaid amounted to £32,
(c) rates and insurance paid in advance, £160,
(d) a bad debts provision equal to 5 per cent of the debtors is to be carried forward,
(e) depreciation is to be provided as follows:

| office equipment | 10% p.a. on cost |
| shop fixtures and fittings | 12½% p.a. on cost |

(f) create a provision for discounts allowed amounting to £34.

Trial Balance, 31st May 19-1

	Dr	Cr
Capital		£10,170
Drawings for the year	£1,480	
Premises at cost	4,000	
Sundry debtors and creditors	1,700	1,070
Stock, 1st June 19-0	2,000	
Salaries	730	
Carriage on purchases	720	
Carriage on sales	200	
Rates and insurance	580	
Purchases and sales	20,220	24,310
Returns	290	140
Advertising	103	
Bad debts	74	
Rent received		160
Office equipment at cost	810	
Shop fixtures and fittings at cost	4,800	
Accumulated provision for depreciation		
Office equipment		200
Shop fixtures and fittings		800
Cash in hand	73	
Bank overdraft		870
Provision for debtors, 1st June 19-0		60
	£37,780	£37,780

CHAPTER XVIII

MOVING TOWARDS ACCOUNTANCY

CAPITAL EMPLOYED

1. Bridging the gap between book-keeping and accountancy.
By the time that the student has reached this stage it is to be
expected that he has a reasonable knowledge of the orderly
manner in which business transactions should be recorded, and,
equally important, he should know the *reasoning* which lies
behind each entry. So far as this goes, so good. Many students,
however, will not be entirely satisfied in merely having acquired
another skill but will wish to make use of it, if that be possible,
in some positive way.

Book-keeping is the foundation upon which all accounting is
based and the field which it can serve is almost unlimited. It is
the tool of the accounting trade and a truly remarkable tool it
is indeed. In this chapter we shall be dealing with certain
results which can be produced by book-keeping enabling
management to become better informed. From such information decisions can be taken regarding future planning of business policy and operational effectiveness which would not
otherwise be possible.

2. The capital needed to start a business. In Chapter II we
considered the *purpose* of the capital a person plans to invest in
a business. At that point in time no business had actually been
created. The point was made in **15** that the one essential requirement to *start* a business from scratch is *money*. In **16** it
was pointed out that this money was not being made available
for it to lay dormant. It was being provided to meet certain
essential expenses such as the purchase of a *place* from which
the business could be carried on, the provision of proper equipment and a stock of goods to sell. Thus, the money which was
to be invested would be described as the capital employed in
the business, *i.e.* at the time the business is being formed. This
is an important concept because as soon as trading commences
additional matters will have to be brought into the calculation.

EXAMPLE

Peter Greenwood started a business with £10,000 which he
paid into a bank account in the name of the business. With this
money he purchased a fourteen year lease on some premises at a
cost of £4,200; fixtures and equipment for £1,750 and a stock of
goods which cost £4,000.

After the above transactions had been completed the opening
balance sheet of the business would have appeared as follows:

Capital Account		Fixed Assets		
Peter Greenwood £10,000		Lease of premises		£4,200
		Fixtures and fittings		1,750
				£5,950
Current liabilities		Current Assets		
—	—	Stock	£4,000	
		Cash at bank	50	
				4,050
	£10,000			£10,000

From the above balance sheet it is clear that the capital employed amounts to £10,000, *i.e.* the total of *all* of the assets.

3. Capital employed when operating a business. As soon as a
business begins to trade, the capital employed will change. As
goods are sold replacements must be made and if these replacement goods are bought on credit we will have, for a certain
time, a number of unpaid suppliers appearing under the heading of "Current Liabilities" on subsequent balance sheets. The
same position will also apply where creditors for unpaid services, such as electricity, telephone, advertising, etc., arise.
Creditors who supply goods or services for which they have not
been paid are, in effect, lending money to the business temporarily.

EXAMPLE

At the end of Peter Greenwood's first year of trading the
position was that his net profit had amounted to £3,850.
Creditors for goods remaining unpaid were £1,645 while amounts
owing for gas and electric light amounted to £39. He was owed
£1,757 by debtors. Stock at cost stood at £4,410 and the balance
at bank was £302. One-fourteenth (£300) of the cost of the lease
was to be written off and fixtures and equipment were to be de-

preciated by 10 per cent. Greenwood drew cash amounting to £3,590 out of the business for his own personal use.

The balance sheet set out below has been divided into four quadrants labelled A, B, C and D respectively.

A		B	
Capital Account		Fixed Assets	
Balance at start	£10,000	Lease at cost £4,200	
Add: Profit for the		*Less:* Depre-	
year	3,850	ciation 300	
	———		£3,900
	13,850	Fixtures and Equipment	
Less: Drawings	3,590	At cost 1,750	
	———	*Less:*	
	10,260	Written off 175	
		———	1,575

C		D	
Current Liabilities		Current Assets	
Creditors for		Stock	£4,410
goods	£1,645	Debtors	1,757
Creditors for		Cash at bank	302
light	39		
	——— 1,684		——— 6,469
	£11,944		£11,944

The idea behind setting out the balance sheet into the four quadrants is partly for ease of identification of the four main headings normally to be found on a balance sheet, but mostly so that students can relate the type of assets/liabilities to positions on the balance sheet. It will help to clarify certain matters which follow.

4. Capital employed and total funds employed. A glance at the balance sheet above shows that the total of the assets amounts to £11,944. This sum is more than the final balance which appears on the Capital Account, £10,260. The last paragraph of **2**, referring to the balance sheet in the example shown, stated that the *capital employed* constituted the sum of *all* the assets. It must be emphasised that this statement, while being true for the opening of a *new* business, does *not* apply where creditors are owed money for goods or services supplied, as was explained in **3**.

In the balance sheet above we see that the business *owed* £1,684 to various people, *i.e.* those people, suppliers of goods and services, who had not yet been paid and who were, therefore, financing Greenwood's business to that extent. In precisely the same way Greenwood was financing other people or other businesses to the extent of £1,757, the total amount *owed to* his business by the debtors. Naturally enough, it is to be expected that these debts, both owed and owing, will be settled in due course. Suppose that all the debtors paid what they owed. The balance at bank would immediately increase to £2,059 thus enabling Greenwood to pay off the creditors (£1,684 in total), leaving a balance at the bank of £375. The total of all the assets would *then* be £10,260, made up as follows:

Lease	£3,900
Fixtures and equipment	1,575
Stock	4,410
Cash at bank	375
Capital Employed	£10,260

Looking again at the balance sheet we note that the balance appearing on the Capital Account is £10,260 which is the difference between the total of all the assets *less* the total of the current liabilities. Thus we can correctly conclude that the capital employed *once trading has commenced* is no longer simply the sum total of all the assets but the amount shown as the balance on the proprietor's Capital Account, or *total* assets less *current* liabilities.

Turning to the matter of the "total funds employed" or being "used" in a business, we would be right in saying that the total of *all* the assets represented the total funds employed. The balance sheet set out in the previous section gives us the following information:

(*a*) Funds provided by Greenwood:

(i) Cash at the start		£10,000
(ii) Net profit for the year	£3,850	
Less: Drawings	3,590	
		260
		10,260

(b)	Funds provided by suppliers of goods	1,645
(c)	Funds provided by suppliers of services	39

Total Funds Employed	£11,944

It is important that the student appreciates the distinction between the *capital* employed in a business and the *total funds* employed.

5. Loans. The reasons which may require that a business borrows money from outside sources can depend on many factors, none of which concerns us here. We must, however, consider loans in the general context of the money (normally referred to as "capital") a business may require for its general trading purposes.

Broadly speaking, loans fall into the two following categories:

    (a) long-term loans;
    (b) short-term loans.

6. "Long-term" loans. This refers to loans which are not intended to be repaid for a long period, usually years.

A "long-term" loan is normally raised where the proprietor of a business is unable to introduce personally the additional capital which he feels is required. For example, a new machine may be urgently needed but the cost is prohibitive in the present financial situation. So, having reached the limit of his own resources, the proprietor is forced to search for a source of additional finance. His bank may be prepared to help him or he may perhaps be able to interest a friend who has some surplus funds. He could advertise for financial help or possibly turn to a hire-purchase finance house.

Assuming that the cash is forthcoming from one source or another the lender of the money immediately becomes a *creditor* of the business, and, as such, will duly appear on the business balance sheet in that capacity. The money will be absorbed into the general funds of the business and used for whatever purpose it was raised, *e.g.* for the purchase of business premises. It is clear that a loan of this character must fall into the category of *capital*. That is to say, the purpose for which the loan was raised had a similar objective to that for which the

original capital was invested by the owner, *i.e.* for the further
ance of the business. This being the case we can then say tha
such a loan must be regarded as part of the permanent capita
structure of the business (even though it has not been supplied
by the owner) and it *must* appear in quadrant A of the balanc
sheet, the section in which the capital of the business is con
tained. We may therefore as a matter of convenience refer to
quadrant A as the "fixed liabilities" section. The term "fixed"
does not mean that no change will ever take place. This also
applies to fixed assets since they do change. Perhaps the term
"permanent" might be a more satisfactory description.

7. "Short-term" loans.

In **4** it was demonstrated that the
suppliers of goods and services who had not been paid were, in
fact, financing Greenwood's business to the extent of the
amounts which were owing to them. We do not, however
show them as having *loaned* money to the business. They are
regarded as creditors arising out of the normal day-to-day
business operations and, as such, will appear in the balanc
sheet under the heading of "Current Liabilities". Such items
will appear in quadrant C.

There is one type of current liability which is, in fact, re
garded as being a "short-term" loan. This arises where the
bank has permitted the owner to *overdraw* on the business bank
account. In such a case we will show, as a *separate* item, under
the heading of current liabilities "Bank Overdraft" indicating
that a short-term loan of this nature exists.

Attention must be drawn to the fact that many large-scale
businesses (and some not-so-large) tend to operate a permanent
bank overdraft. This sort of arrangement exists as a matter of
convenience so long as the bank is satisfied as to the solvency
of the business and the security of its money. Even though the
amount involved is often relatively large bank *overdrafts* are
not bank *loans*. A loan from a bank is a long-term liability; a
bank overdraft is a short-term liability. The reason for this
difference in treatment is basically that an overdraft *fluctuates*
i.e. the amount owing to the bank moves up or down on a day
to-day basis, and the overdraft facility as it is called may be
withdrawn by the bank should it become nervous or dissatisfied
with the manner in which the business appears to be conducted
It has to be remembered that the bank is using money belong
ing to its own customers to finance, say, Greenwood's over

draft, and if it becomes uneasy with his behaviour it can at once refuse to meet any cheques which he may draw (while he is working on an overdraft).

With a bank loan the circumstances are rather different. The loan, often requiring the approval of the bank's head office, will be entered into for a specific period of time, *e.g.* four years. The bank may require some security to be "charged" to it. This is a legal procedure whereby a certain asset, *e.g.* the premises which the business owns, may be lawfully taken over by the bank and sold if the borrower fails to meet his periodic repayments of the loan. Generally speaking, however, a bank would not "call in" a loan except as a last resort.

WORKING CAPITAL

8. The meaning of the expression "working capital". The term "working capital" is used normally to indicate the amount of *surplus funds* a business *has available at any time* to enable it to meet demands which require *immediate* settlement. Creditors may perhaps be pressing for money which is due to them or salaries must be paid at the end of each month. It is clear that a business must have sufficient cash available for payments such as these.

9. Current assets. This expression is used to denote those assets which are convertible into money in the short term. Most of them change from day to day. Consider cash at bank or cash in hand; stock is continually on the move: some of it being sold while fresh stocks come in; debtors may pay their accounts but take a discount, thus leaving a slightly different position in the amount of current assets. They are sometimes called *circulating capital* because they are constantly in motion. The normal items which are regarded as current assets are as follows:

(*a*) Stock in trade.
(*b*) Debtors.
(*c*) Payments in advance (a form of debtors).
(*d*) Cash at the bank.
(*e*) Cash in hand.

It is easy to see that with the exception of payments in

advance, assets which fall into the list set out above are subject
to continual movement. Even amounts of money which have
been prepaid, such as premiums for insurance cover, will
diminish on a day-to-day basis.

10. Current liabilities. The title "current liabilities" is given
to those creditors which a business must satisfy by *a payment in
cash* in the very near future. The most usual headings under
which current liabilities fall are:

(*a*) Trade creditors, *i.e.* for goods supplied for resale.
(*b*) Accrued expenses, *i.e.* for services supplied.
(*c*) Income tax which is payable within the current year.
(*d*) Dividends declared (in the case of a limited company)
which will be payable almost immediately.
(*e*) Bank overdrafts.

11. Calculating the working capital of a business. This can be
obtained by means of a very simple calculation. Theoretically,
by subtracting the total of the current liabilities (quadrant C in
3) from the total of the current assets (quadrant D) we obtain
the working capital. In practice it may not be quite as simple
because in the event of an emergency it might prove impossible
to obtain all the money owed by the debtors at the very time it
was needed. Similarly, to raise the money shown as being the
value of the stock may be a hopeless task if the cash is required
urgently.

EXAMPLE
The balance sheet of William Todhunter at 31st August,
19–8, was as under:

Capital Account			Fixed Assets		
W. Todhunter		£17,000	Premises		£12,000
			Plant		2,400
			Equipment		760
					15,160
Current Liabilities			Current Assets		
Goods	£980		Stock	1,420	
Accrued			Debtors	1,180	
expenses	92		Cash at bank	312	
		1,072			2,912
		£18,072			£18,072

To obtain the figure of working capital all we have to do is to subtract the total of the current liabilities from the total of the current assets. In the example set out above we have:

Current Assets	£2,912
Less: Current liabilities	1,072
WORKING CAPITAL	£1,840

To find the *capital employed* we must take the total of all of the assets and deduct from this the current liabilities, as under:

Total assets at 31st December 19–8	£18,072
Less: current liabilities	1,072
CAPITAL EMPLOYED	£17,000

12. Working Capital ratio. It is appropriate at this point to mention a ratio which is used as a quick and convenient means of assessing the ability of a business to pay its debts within the normal period expected in the particular trade. For example creditors may require payment within six weeks of the date of purchase whereas debtors may expect to be given two months credit. No hard and fast rule as to the length of the period of credit can be laid down as circumstances can vary so very much.

The "working capital" ratio, as it is called (or sometimes the "current" ratio), is obtained thus:

$$\text{Working Capital ratio} = \frac{\text{Current assets}}{\text{Current liabilities}}$$

Conventionally, a 2:1 ratio is regarded as being desirable.

EXAMPLE

The summarised balance sheets of John Stillson at the end of 19–3 and 19–4 were as follows:

	31st December 19–3 £	31st December 19–4 £
Buildings at cost	80,000	100,000
Plant at cost less depreciation	51,600	65,400
Motor vehicles at cost less depreciation	7,100	8,400
Stock	17,150	24,370
Debtors	22,280	15,610
Cash balance	740	220
	£178,870	£214,000

	£	£
Capital account	158,785	161,840
Loan	—	20,000
Creditors for purchases and expenses	12,085	23,660
Bank overdraft	8,000	8,500
	£178,870	£214,000

Required:

(a) State the amount of the current assets, the current liabilities, the working capital and the working capital ratio at 31st December 19–3 and at 31st December 19–4. Present your answer in the following form:

Current assets:
Current liabilities:
Working capital:
Working capital ratio:

(b) Comment briefly on the changes that have taken place during 19–4 in Stillson's working capital.

(R.S.A. adapted)

SOLUTION

John Stillson

	19–3	19–4
(a) Current assets	40,170	40,200
less: Current liabilities	20,085	32,160
Working capital	20,085	8,040

WORKING CAPITAL RATIO $\dfrac{\text{Current assets}}{\text{Current liabilities}} = \dfrac{40,170}{20,085} : \dfrac{40,200}{32,160}$

Ratio = 2·00 : 1·25

(b) The *total* current assets has remained practically unchanged but in 19–4 the liquid position deteriorated very much as can be seen in the working capital ratio. While the bank overdraft increased by only £500 the amount owing to suppliers and other creditors nearly doubled, *i.e.* an increase of £11,575. Thus, the amounts owing to outsiders increased by more than £12,000.

A study of the individual current assets as between 19–3 and 19–4 tells the story of danger ahead with approximately 5/8th of their total value being tied up in stock (the most immediately unrealisable of the current assets).

FLOW OF FUNDS

13. Flow of funds statements. Various statements can be produced showing from what sources funds flow into a business *i.e.* from what origins they have been generated and in what way this money has been spent. The essence of such statements is to show *in some detail* both the sources and the uses to which these funds have been put because it is only by pinpointing such matters that interested parties are able to make proper judgments. This, of course, applies particularly to the management of limited companies where the ownership may be widely spread. It also applies to banks which frequently lend money to businesses and clearly have a considerable interest in the way they are being managed and how their money is being spent. The terms "funds flow" and "cash flow" means the same thing.

When dealing with individual items students very often have difficulty in deciding whether an item is a "source of funds" or an "application of funds." This may seem a strange thing to say but we are dealing with an area where clear thinking is vital. When, for example, we find that the creditors of a business are owed more at the year end than they were owed at the start we do not tend to think of this as a "source" of funds. Yet it should be treated as such. The reasoning is that if we owe more to our creditors at the end of the year than we did at the beginning we are making use of *their* money instead of having had to use *our own*. We have obtained goods without having given anything in exchange—hence it is a source of funds. We should commit to memory the following:

   (*a*) Source of funds:
      (i) reduction in an asset.
      (ii) increase in a liability.
   (*b*) Use of funds:
      (i) increase in an asset.
      (ii) decrease in a liability.

The following aide-memoire is offered in the hope that it may help to lock matters securely in the mind of the student The words FRAIL and EARLY are used not because they relate to the subject-matter but because it is well-known that such mnemonics do, in fact, work.

(a) Source of funds: (b) Use of funds:

F = Financed by   E = Enlargement
R = Reduction in   (increase) in
A = Asset value   A = Asset value
I = Increase in   R = Reduction in
L = Liability $\left.\begin{array}{l}L\\Y\end{array}\right\}$ = Liability

It is important to appreciate that *two* balance sheets are
always required, *i.e.* at the start and finish of the period (of
whatever length) under review.

SOURCES OF FUNDS

14. The generation of working capital. Working capital, *i.e.*
funds, may be introduced into a business by means of loans,
fresh capital and even the sale of some of its fixed assets. However, the most usual way by which funds may be increased is
by the business making a profit on its trading.

EXAMPLE

A business was started with capital in cash amounting to
£1,000. Fixtures costing £100 were purchased before trading
started. The Balance Sheet would have appeared as follows:

BALANCE SHEET AS AT 1ST JANUARY

Capital	£1,000	Fixtures	100
		Bank	900
	£1,000		£1,000

The transactions for the first year of trading were as follows:

Cash purchases	£12,000
Cash sales	£15,000
Expenses (all paid for in cash)	£1,400

All takings were banked and all payments were made by
cheque. There was no stock on hand at the end of the year.

Cash Book (Bank Account)

Capital A/c	£1,000	Fixtures A/c	£100
Sales A/c	15,000	Purchases A/c	12,000
		Expenses A/c	1,400
		Balance	2,500
	£16,000		£16,000

Trading and Profit and Loss Account

Purchases	£12,000	Sales	£15,000
Gross profit	3,000		
	£15,000		£15,000
Expenses	£1,400	Gross profit	£3,000
Net Profit	1,600		
	£3,000		£3,000

BALANCE SHEET AS AT 31ST DECEMBER

Capital A/c	£1,000	Fixtures	£100
Add: net profit	1,600	Bank	2,500
	£2,600		£2,600

After the purchase of the fixtures for £100 there was left the sum of £900 as working capital at the start.

All of the profit was realised, *i.e.* all transactions were on a cash basis, and so the net profit of £1,600 can be seen to have been received by the business in cash. To the balance of £900 cash at bank on 1st January there has been added during the year the sum of £1,600, the profit realised in cash, which gives a closing balance of £2,500 cash at the bank on 31st December. Thus the working capital amounts to £2,500, since there are no current liabilities and the only current asset is the cash at the bank. Thus the difference between the opening and closing working capital (£900–£2,500) is £1,600, which of course corresponds to the exact amount of net profit made during the year.

If the business had conducted its operations on a credit basis instead of for cash the same result would apply, since instead of collecting cash from the customers for goods sold a number of debtors would appear on the books. Debtors are, of course, current assets in the same way as cash. Suppose, then, purely for the sake of illustrating the point, that all the sales had been on credit and that no cash had been received, the net profit would have been exactly the same, *i.e.* £1,600. If we assume that all the transactions, both buying and selling, were on credit the Balance Sheet would appear as under:

BALANCE SHEET AS AT 31ST DECEMBER

Capital A/c	£1,000	Fixed assets	
Add: net profit	1,600	Fixtures	£100
	2,600	Current assets	
Current liabilities		Debtors	£15,000
Creditors for		Bank	900
goods	£12,000		———
Accrued			15,900
expenses	1,400		
	———		
	13,400		
	———		———
	£16,000		£16,000

Subtracting *current liabilities* of £13,400 from current assets of £15,900 we are left with £2,500 as the *working capital*, as before.

15. Interpreting balance sheet changes. When we try to explain the changes which have taken place in the items of one balance sheet and the next it is not always an easy matter to *grasp the significance* of those changes. What is needed is a series of statements which gather together the details of those changes and *those changes only*. Anything else is irrelevant.

It is suggested that the series of statements should be in the following pattern:

    (*a*) Two columns headed respectively "sources of funds" and "use of funds" in which will be shown the *individual* changes in *all* assets and liabilities.

    (*b*) Two columns (*not* headed) showing the *individual* changes in those items concerned with *working capital*.

    (*c*) A statement setting out the calculations of working capital at the *start* of the period and at the *end* of the period and giving the figure of the difference.

    (*d*) A reconciliation setting out in detail those items which have brought about the difference.

FUNDS STATEMENTS

16. Preparing a funds statement. It is essential that the balance sheets of at least two *consecutive* years are available for

purposes of comparison. Ideally, they
form, although not necessarily so. The
makes comparison much easier especiall
individual items.

EXAMPLE

The balance sheets of George Green's
years ending 31st December 19–5 and 19–6 respectively, are as
follows:

	31st December 19–5		31st December 19–6	
	£	£	£	£
Fixed assets at cost	25,000		43,800	
less: depreciation	8,700		12,400	
	——	16,300	——	31,400
Current assets				
Stock	12,260		18,724	
Debtors	9,472		14,628	
Bank	8,356		145	
	——	30,088	——	33,497
		£46,388		£64,897
Capital		20,000		20,000
Retained profit (after deducting drawings)		10,248		16,854
		30,248		36,854
Loan from B. Brown		—		10,000
Current liabilities		16,140		18,043
		£46,388		£64,897

Required:

(a) a statement of funds flow;

(b) a brief comment on the financial policy followed by
George Green during 19–6.   (R.S.A.)

Before passing on to the suggested solution let us remind ourselves of what we have to do when analysing the two balance
sheets.

(a) Changes to be shown in *all* assets and liabilities (not
merely those which comprise the working capital).

(b) Changes in the composition of the working capital in
each balance sheet.

(c) A calculation of the total working capital for each of the two years.

(d) A reconciliation of the opening and closing working capital.

An important benefit arising from carrying out the above procedures is that a cross-check is automatically provided which can be of great help in ensuring that one's workings are correct.

SUGGESTED SOLUTION

George Green Ltd.

(a) Individual Changes in all Assets and Liabilities

	Source of funds	Use of funds
Fixed Assets purchased: increase		15,100
Stock: increase		6,464
Debtors: increase		5,156
Bank: decrease	8,211	
Profit	6,606	
Loan from B. Brown	10,000	
Creditors	1,903	
	£26,720	£26,720

(b) Individual Changes in Working Capital

Stock		6,464
Debtors		5,156
Creditors	1,903	
Bank	8,211	
net use of funds (as shown in (c) below)	1,506	
	£11,620	£11,620

(c) Working Capital

	19–5	19–6
	£	£
Current assets	30,088	33,497
Less: Current liabilities	16,140	18,043
Working Capital	at start of year £13,948	at end of year £15,454
Increase in Working Capital	£1,506	

(as in (b) above)

(d) *Reconciliation*

		£
Working Capital at start (as at (c) above)		13,948
Add : Profit for year	6,606	
Depreciation	3,700	
Loan from B. Brown	10,000	
		20,306
		34,254
Less : Purchase of fixed assets		18,800
Working Capital at close (as at (c) above)		£15,454

PROGRESS TEST 18

Theory

1. What is the difference between the capital employed (*a*) before a business starts trading and (*b*) once it has started trading? **(2, 3)**

2. What do you understand by the expression "total funds employed"? **(4)**

3. Distinguish between long-term loans and short-term loans. **(5, 6, 7)**

4. What is the difference between a bank loan and a bank overdraft? **(7)**

5. Define "working capital." **(8)**

6. What items normally fall under the heading of "current assets" and "current liabilities"? **(9, 10)**

7. How is working capital calculated? **(11)**

8. What is meant by "working capital ratio"? **(12)**

9. "Flow of funds" is a term very much used in business. It is often spoken of as "cash flow." Give two examples of where funds which enter a business originate and two examples showing how such funds are applied (used) in a business. **(13)**

Practice

10. The balance sheets of Chalmers and Son at 31st December, 19–1, and 31st December, 19–2 are as follows:

	19–1		19–2	
	£	£	£	£
Fixed assets				
Plant at cost	40,000		60,000	
Less: depreciation	18,300		24,500	
		21,700		35,500
Transport at cost	5,000		6,000	
Less: depreciation	2,400		3,900	
		2,600		2,100
Current assets				
Stock	7,138		10,242	
Debtors	5,209		7,116	
Bank	4,163		4,295	
		16,510		21,653
		£40,810		£59,253
Capital account		31,332		43,119
Bank loan		—		5,000
Current liabilities		9,478		11,134
		£40,810		£59,253

You are required to redraft these two balance sheets to show the working capital and the capital employed at the 31st December, 19–1 and at the 31st December, 19–2. (R.S.A.)

11. The following is the balance sheet of Brambell & Co., a manufacturing concern:

BALANCE SHEET AS AT 31ST DECEMBER, 19–0

	£		£
Capital Account	31,000	Freehold buildings	15,000
Bank Loan	10,000	Plant and Machinery	10,500
Creditors	8,000	Stock	8,500
		Debtors	9,000
		Bank Balance	6,000
	£49,000		£49,000

You are required to calculate:
  (a) capital employed;
  (b) current assets;
  (c) current liabilities;
  (d) working capital.

12. The summarised balance sheets of Murlow and Sons at the end of 19–4 and 19–5 are as follows:

	31st December 19–4 £	31st December 19–5 £
Buildings at cost	82,000	92,000
Plant at cost, *less* depreciation	51,500	69,500
Motor vehicles at cost, *less* depreciation	8,700	9,400
Stock	17,500	27,300
Debtors	14,300	15,100
Bank balance	10,200	2,600
	£184,200	£215,900

Capital after deducting drawings	163,200	168,900
Loan from S. Black	—	17,000
Creditors for purchases and expenses	12,500	19,500
Bank overdraft	8,500	10,500
	£184,200	£215,900

Required:

(*a*) A statement of the amount of the current assets, the current liabilities, the working capital and the working capital ratio at 31st December, 19–4, and at 31st December 19–5. Present your answer in the following form:

	19–4	19–5
Current assets	—	—
Current liabilities	—	—
Working Capital	—	—
Working capital ratio	—	—

(*b*) Comment briefly on the implications of the changes that have taken place during 19–5 in Murlow's working capital.

(Institute of Bankers)

13. The balance sheets of N. Tree's business for the years ended 31st December, 19–8 and 31st December, 19–9, were:

	31st December 19–8	31st December 19–9
	£	£
Capital A/c	5,420	5,420
Add: Net profit for 19–9		8,690
		14,110
Less: Drawings for 19–9		4,355
		9,755
Bank Loan	10,000	4,500
Creditors	4,200	5,050
	£19,620	£19,305

		31st December 19–8		31st December 19–9
Fixed Assets				
Buildings		6,000		6,000
Plant (after depreciation)		3,000		4,200
Motor Vans (after depreciation)		1,750		1,400
Current Assets				
Stocks	3,250		4,175	
Debtors	2,840		2,620	
Cash at bank	2,780		910	
		8,870		7,705
		£19,620		£19,305

You are required to show:

(*a*) the changes in all the assets and liabilities differentiating between sources and uses;

(*b*) the individual changes in assets and liabilities relating to the working capital;

(*c*) calculations of the working capital showing the net difference between the two amounts;

(*d*) a reconciliation showing how the difference came about.

EXAMINATION TECHNIQUE

Preparation

The only road to certain success in accountancy examinations is for the student to have acquired a *thoroughly sound knowledge* of double-entry book-keeping. Unless his knowledge is soundly based, he will forever find himself in a twilight world where some things are understood dimly and where a great deal is completely incomprehensible. Many students regrettably fall into this category and, as a result, fail miserably in their efforts to master the subject.

It must be pointed out that to have a thoroughly sound knowledge of the principles of book-keeping the student must first of all know *why* things are done. It can be claimed with some justification that book-keeping is a logical discipline and this is manifest to anyone who really understands book-keeping. When one accepts that book-keeping *is* logical, it follows that *reasoning* can be applied to its problems. This is the key to making good progress. There is, indeed, a basic reason for everything that is done in book-keeping, and since the principles of book-keeping are applied one hundred per cent to accountancy problems it follows that without a thorough knowledge of the fundamentals, examination success will be very hard to attain.

There is a second ingredient which is required for success in accountancy examinations. This is *practice* in the working of problems. Furthermore, this practice must be a continuous exercise. In the months of preparation before the examination, a very great deal of the student's time must be devoted to the working of problems. Accountancy is not a subject which can be mastered just by reading. It is an intensely practical subject and practical subjects can only be mastered by *constant* practice. Ideally, at least two hours a day for five days a week should be spent on working practical problems in accountancy during the months of preparation for your examination. For this you should acquire as many past examination papers *with worked solutions* as you can. It does not matter which examining body's papers you obtain; they will all afford you the opportunity for plentiful and varied practice. (Quite a number of organisations specialise in supplying past examination papers and they usually advertise in the professional journals.)

In addition, you should obtain *several* books on accountancy.

Do not rely on just one book. One finds that some books deal with specific aspects of accountancy better than others. Again, the approach of one author may appeal to one student but not to another. Hence, a little variety in your textbooks may prove to be of great value.

At the examination

In these hints on examination technique, two assumptions have been made. These are:

(a) that the student has covered the syllabus and
(b) that he has a reasonable grasp of the principles of the subject.

To these a third could well be added, *i.e.* that no student can reasonably hope to achieve 100 per cent of the available marks, neither is it necessary for him to do so to pass the examination. This is not only a comforting thought but it is also common sense and should be borne in mind when in the examination hall. It is better to answer some of the questions *really well* and gain sufficient marks in that way than to answer all inadequately and probably fail.

Most of the professional bodies require the candidate to answer five questions in accountancy examinations. It is only very occasionally that the answers to six questions are called for. Some bodies give a choice, *e.g.* seven questions are set with five to be answered.

Choice. Where a choice of questions is offered, the student should be very careful to answer *only one of the alternatives*.

It is by no means uncommon to find students disregarding this point. Whether they do so in error or because they find that they can answer both, it must be pointed out emphatically that they will be credited only with the marks attaching to *one* of their answers. Which one will depend upon the view taken by the examiner. He may adopt the view that the first one dealt with by the candidate is the one which is to count. On the other hand, he may be more charitable and take the trouble to mark both answers, crediting the candidate with the higher scoring answer. Both questions would, of course, carry the same possible maximum mark.

Allocation of marks. In accountancy examinations, marks are allocated to certain parts of the answers. It is most important for the student to realise this. A simple illustration will make the point easier to appreciate.

Suppose a question set out the trial balance of a firm and beneath it a number of adjustments which had to be incorporated in the final accounts and balance sheet. The total marks for the question might be 25.

Three marks might be awarded for dealing correctly with the provision for doubtful debts, one mark for deducting a pre-payment from the Profit and Loss Account charge for insurance and a fifth mark for entering the balance under current assets in the balance sheet. Two marks might be given to the correct treatment of goods on sale or return in the Trading Account and yet another mark for the inclusion of the item in the closing stock in the balance sheet. This pattern will be continued throughout the remainder of the question. Finally, an award of, say, three marks might be given for presentation.

Many students seem to think that because they have managed to balance both sides of the balance sheet they will score full marks. This is far from reality. Conversely, many feel that because they have not balanced they will score no marks. This again is far from true.

Time wasted. If the student has prepared himself reasonably well for the examination, he will expect to find some questions, at least, of a type that he recognises and which he can make a fair attempt at answering. Often, however, having worked through a question, he finds that he must have gone wrong at some point since his final answer is clearly incorrect.

There is a great danger here that he will spend an inordinate amount of time trying to locate his mistake. At this stage he should do no more than quickly run over his answer, making a pencil cross against any points of doubt—unless, of course, he can see the cause of his error at once. In this latter case the necessary adjusting entries should be made. It is more likely, however, that his error will not be immediately apparent and, in that case, his best plan is to leave matters as they stand and *not waste any time at all* at this stage.

Many students have failed examinations because they wasted a vast amount of time in a fruitless effort to discover an error. In so many cases its discovery would have made only a very small difference to the number of marks earned.

If the mistake is not immediately apparent, *move to the next question at once.*

Allocating time to questions. If you have a watch, place it on the desk in front of you.

The normal maximum marks for an accountancy paper is 100. The normal time allowance is three hours and this allows nearly two minutes per mark. Nearly every professional examination shows the number of marks allocated to each question, so you can make a rough calculation of the number of minutes that you can afford to devote to each question.

It is at this point that your attention is drawn to the opening remarks of this section, *i.e.* that none but the most gifted student can hope to score full marks. If you score sixty you will be sure of passing. Are you capable of scoring sixty? Do the questions appear to give you that hope? Can you answer four of the five well, or only three? These questions can only be answered by the candidate with the examination paper in front of him. If the reply to the first question is favourable, then take care to allocate the appropriate amount of time per question before settling down to work. But remember that if, for example, you answer four questions out of five, your sixty marks must be earned from a total of, perhaps, eighty possible marks only. It would be wise, there-fore, to leave half an hour at the end for going on to another ques-tion to earn a few bonus marks and for "polishing up" your answers.

By adopting this technique, quite a lot of the "pressure" will be eased. The result will almost certainly be that a far better paper will be handed in than would otherwise be the case.

SUGGESTED ANSWERS TO TEST QUESTIONS

Chapter II

5

Capital Account—M. Lomax

		Cash Invested in Business A/c	£3,000

Cash Invested in Business Account

Capital A/c	£3,000	Boyds Bank A/c	£3,000

Boyds Bank Account

Cash Invested in Business A/c	£3,000		

BALANCE SHEET OF "LOMAX MOTORS"

Liabilities
Capital Account—M. Lomax   £3,000

Assets
Boyds Bank Account   £3,000

6

Capital Account—R. Ferguson

		Cash Invested in Business A/c	£3,250

Cash Invested in Business Account

Capital A/c	£3,250	Redland Bank A/c	£3,250

Redland Bank Account

Cash Invested in Business A/c	£3,250		

BALANCE SHEET OF "FERGIE'S FISH BAR"

Liabilities

Capital Account—R. Ferguson £3,250

Assets

Redland Bank Account £3,250

17

Capital Account—N. Bridge

		Southern Bank A/c	£4,000
		Southern Bank A/c	800
			£4,800

Southern Bank Account

Capital A/c	£4,000		
Capital A/c	800		
	£4,800		

BALANCE SHEET OF "THE FRUIT SHOP"

Liabilities

Capital Account—N. Bridge £4,800

Assets

Southern Bank Account £4,800

NOTE: In this example Cash Invested in Business Account has been omitted and the double entry between the Bank Account and the Capital Account has been made *direct*. This practice should be followed from this point on when working problems.

Chapter III

9

Capital Account—H. Webster

		Bank A/c	£5,000

Bank Account

Capital A/c	£5,000	Landlord's A/c	£750
		Shop Fittings A/c	1,000
		Purchase of Goods A/c	
		(Stock)	3,000
		Balance c/d	250
	£5,000		£5,000
Balance b/d	250		

Landlord's Account

Bank A/c	£750		

Shop Fittings Account

Bank A/c	£1,000		

Purchase of Goods Account (i.e. Stock)

Bank A/c	£3,000		

BALANCE SHEET

Liabilities

Capital Account—H. Webster		£5,000

Assets

Shop fittings	£1,000	
Stock	3,000	
Debtors—(landlord for rent paid in advance)	750	
Bank	250	
		£5,000

Capital Account—P. Jennings

Bank A/c	£500	Bank A/c	£10,000

Chalkleys Bank Account

Capital A/c	£10,000	Shop Premises A/c	£5,750
		Motor Van A/c	425
		Shop Premises A/c (legal costs)	150
		Shop Fittings A/c	600
		Purchase of Goods A/c (stock)	2,300
		Capital A/c (personal drawings)	500
			9,725
		Balance c/d	275
	£10,000		£10,000
Balance b/d	£275		

Shop Premises Account

Bank A/c	£5,750		
„ „ (legal costs)	150		
	£5,900		

Motor Van Account

Bank A/c	£425	

Shop Fittings Account

Bank A/c	£600	

Purchase of Goods Account (i.e. Stock)

Bank A/c	£2,300	

BALANCE SHEET

Liabilities
  Capital Account—P. Jennings
  Cash introduced at start   £10,000
    Less Cash withdrawn for personal use   500
                                                  ———————   £9,500

Assets
  Fixed assets
    Shop premises   £5,900
    Shop fittings   600
    Motor van   425
                                                  ———————   £6,925

  Current assets
    Stock   2,300
    Bank   275
                                                                        £2,575

                                                                        £9,500

NOTE: The assets are placed in *order of realisability* with fixed assets at the top of the balance sheet. Those most unlikely to be disposed of are placed at the top then follow those which may be more easily sold. We finish with the current assets starting with stock and concluding with cash at bank.

This is the modern method of presentation and although there is no particular objection to listing entries in reverse order, *i.e.* starting with cash at bank, it is regarded as old-fashioned.

Chapter IV

5

Bank Account					Cash Account			
Capital A/c	£400	Purchases A/c	£300		Capital A/c	£20	Purchases A/c	£18
Cash A/c	60	Cash A/c	20		Bank A/c	20	Bank A/c	
Sales A/c	150	Purchases A/c	200		Sales A/c	63	(takings	
		Rent A/c	20		Sales A/c	35	paid in)	60
			———				Sundry Exps.	
			540				A/c	4
		Balance c/d	70				Capital A/c	
							(drawings)	30
	———		———					———
	£610		£610					112
Balance b/d	70						Balance c/d	26
						£138		£138
					Balance b/d	£26		

NOTE: The item on 4th March, "Cashed cheque for office expenses," is money which has been drawn from the bank *for the purpose of putting the Cash Account in funds* to meet any future expenses which have to be paid for in cash. It has been found that many beginners, *instead of debiting the Cash Account*, open an Office Expenses Account, and debit the money thereto. They then leave this account with a debit balance standing and make no further entries in the account. When they come to prepare their final accounts (see next chapter) and balance sheets they do not know what to do with this item.

6

Bank Account

July 1	Capital A/c	£1,000	July 2	Shop Fittings A/c	£75
13	Cash A/c	145	3	Rent A/c	120
			4	Purchases A/c	248
			5	Cash A/c	25
			15	Capital A/c (drawings)	30
					498
			15	Balance c/d	647
		£1,145			£1,145
	Balance b/d	£647			

Cash Account

July 5	Bank A/c	£25	July 8	Purchases A/c	£45
6	Sales A/c	67	10	Wrapping Paper A/c	8
9	Sales A/c	37	12	Wages A/c	12
11	Sales A/c	64	13	Bank A/c	145
13	Sales A/c	44			210
			15	Balance c/d	27
		£237			£237
	Balance b/d	£27			

Chapter V

ANALYSED PETTY CASH BOOK

Date	Receipts	Description	Payments	Fares	Postages	Cleaning	Stationery	Donations	Sundries
May 1	£20·00	Bank							
1		Stamps	£2·00		£2·00				
2		Fares	1·00	£1·00					
2		Donation	0·50					£0·50	
3		Stationery	3·50				£3·50		
4		Stationery	2·75				2·75		
4		Sundries	2·75						£2·75
5		Cleaning	0·75			£0·75			
6		Wages	5·00			5·00			
6		Fares	0·80	0·80					
			£19·05	£1·80	£2·00	£5·75	£6·25	£0·50	£2·75
6		Balance c/d	0·95						
	£20·00		£20·00						
8	0·95	Balance b/d							
8	£19·05	Bank							

Chapter VI

Entries in the ledger of "The Sports Shop":

Capital Account—S. Leigh

		Bank A/c	£3,500

Bank Account

Capital A/c	£3,500	Shop Fittings A/c	£625
		,, ,, ,,	370
		Purchase of Goods A/c	2,360
			3,355
		Balance c/d	145
	£3,500		£3,500
Balance b/d	£145		

Shop Fittings Account

Bank A/c	£625	
,,	370	
	£995	

Purchase of Goods Account

Bank A/c	£2,360	

BALANCE SHEET

Liabilities
    Capital Account—S. Leigh   £3,50~~~

Assets
    Shop fittings   £99~
    Stock of goods   2,36~
    Bank   14~

                                    £3,50~

7

Stage 1

We must begin by opening those ledger accounts which formed
the balance sheet in Question 6 and enter therein the appropriate
amounts. In this way we make certain that the first period of
trading starts off with a set of ledger accounts which are "in
balance."

Bank Account		*Capital Account*	
Balance b/f £145			Balance b/f £3,50~

Shop Fittings Account		*Purchase of Goods Account*	
Balance b/f £995		Balance b/f £2,360	

Thus the total of the three debit balances amounts to £3,500
which, of course, exactly equals the one credit balance, *i.e.* the
Capital Account.

Stage 2

We now proceed to enter the transactions in the appropriate accounts as follows:

Bank Account

May 1	Balance (from stage 1)	£145	May 6	Advertising A/c	£21
16	Sales A/c	1,200	12	Stationery A/c	15
31	Sales A/c	1,778	17	Purchase of Goods A/c	63
			22	Rent A/c	50
			26	Wages A/c	40
					189
			31	Balance c/d	2,934
		£3,123			£3,123
	Balance b/d	£2,934			

Advertising Account		*Stationery Account*	
Bank A/c £21		Bank A/c £15	

Purchase of Goods Account		*Rent Account*	
Balance (from Stage 1) £2,360		Bank A/c £50	
Bank A/c 63			
£2,423			

Sales Account		*Wages Account*	
	Bank A/c £1,200	Bank A/c £40	
	„ „ 1,778		
	£2,978		

Note that in this stage we brought forward from Stage 1 the balances on the Bank Account and on the Purchase of Goods Account.

Stage 3

Having completed the postings from the Bank Account we now take out a trial balance in order to check the arithmetical accuracy of the entries as well as the additions.

TRIAL BALANCE

	Debit	Credit
Capital A/c (Stage 1)		£3,500
Shop Fittings A/c (Stage 1)	£995	
Advertising A/c (Stage 2)	21	
Purchase of Goods A/c (Stage 2)	2,423	
Sales A/c (Stage 2)		2,978
Bank A/c	2,934	
Stationery A/c (Stage 2)	15	
Rent A/c (Stage 2)	50	
Wages A/c (Stage 2)	40	
	£6,478	£6,478

Stage 4

With the agreement of the trial balance we will now construct the final accounts and the balance sheet.

Trading Account

Purchase of goods	£2,423	Sales	£2,978
Gross profit	555		
	£2,978		£2,978

Profit and Loss Account

Advertising	£21	Gross profit	£555
Stationery	15		
Rent	50		
Wages	40		
	126		
Net profit (to be transferred to the Capital Account)	429		
	£555		£555

Capital Account

Balance from Stage 1	£3,500
Profit and Loss A/c (net profit)	429
	£3,929

NOTE: It is not the usual practice to show the Capital Account *between* the Profit and Loss Account and the balance sheet. It has been entered here to make sure that the student sees exactly what happens to the net profit.

BALANCE SHEET AS AT 31st MAY

Liabilities

Capital Account		
Balance at 1st May	£3,500	
Add Profit for the period	429	
		£3,929

Assets

Shop fittings	£995
Cash at bank	2,934
	£3,929

Chapter VII

7

Gross profit, £20. Net profit, £14.
Balance sheet: Capital, £30 + net profit, £14 = £44
    Equipment, £17 + cash, £27 = £44

8

Gross profit, £25. Net profit, £19.
Balance sheet: Capital, **£44** + net profit, £19 — drawings,
    £7 = **£56**

Equipment, £17 + £5 =	£22
Cash =	£34
	£56

Chapter VIII

11

Gross profit, £82. Net profit, £40. Balance sheet totals, £470.
Bank Account balance, £147. Capital Account (£450 + £40 — £20)
= £470.

12

Bank balance, £1,196. Cost of sales, £495. Gross profit, £254. Net profit, £187. Balance sheet totals, £2,527. Gross profit percentage = 33·9.

13

Bank balance, £2,089. Cost of sales, £906. Gross profit, £459. Net profit, £367. Balance sheet totals, £2,844. Gross profit percentage = 33·6.

14

Opening stock	6,000 at £2 each	£12,000
Purchases	42,000 at £2·25 each	94,500
		106,500
Less Closing stock— 5,000 at £22·5 each		11,250
Cost of goods sold		£95,250

Sales (number of articles)

Opening stock	6,000	
Purchases	42,000	
	48,000	
Less Closing stock	5,000	
Number of articles sold	43,000 at £3 each	£129,000
Less Cost of sales (as above)		95,250
Gross profit		£33,750

15

Trading Account

Opening stock	£1,250	Sales	£20,780
Purchases	14,200		
	15,450		
Less Closing stock			
Costs of goods sold			
Gross profit (30% of sales)	6,234		
	£20,780		£20,780

The gross profit (30% of £20,780) = £6,234. This is placed in the Trading Account and by subtracting it from the sales we find that the cost of goods sold is £14,546. This figure is then deducted from the total of the opening stock and the purchases leaving £904, which must be the value of the closing stock.

Average stock = £1,077.   Cost of sales = £14,546.
Rate of stock turnover = 13·5.

16

Trading Account

Opening stock	£904	Sales	£25,690
Purchases	18,481		
	19,385		
Less Closing stock	1,402		
Cost of goods sold	17,983		
Gross profit (30%)	7,707		
	£25,690		£25,690

Rate of stock turnover
$$\frac{\text{Cost of sales}}{\text{Average stock}} \frac{£17,983}{£1,153} = 15·6.$$

17

Trading Account

Opening stock			Sales		
(1,300 units at £10)		£13,000	(4,700 units at £15)		£70,500
Purchases:			Closing stock:		
1,000 units at £10	£10,000		200 units at £6	£1,200	
1,200 units at £9	10,800		800 units at £8	6,400	
900 units at £7	6,300		600 units at £8	4,800	
500 units at £6	3,000				12,400
800 units at £9	7,200		1,600 units		
600 units at £8	4,800				
		42,100			
		55,100			
Gross profit		27,800			
		£82,900			£82,900

NOTE: As prices were expected to become stable at around £8 per unit, henceforth we should value the 800 units purchased at a cost of £9 each on 23rd November at £8 per item when calculating the value of the closing stock.

Stock is valued, almost without exception, at *cost price o*
current market price. The *lower* of these two prices is the one whic
should be applied when valuing stock for inclusion in the Tradin
Account and in the balance sheet.

In the problem we have 200 units, which were purchased o
17th September at £6 each, still unsold. Since the current marke
price on 31st December was £8, these 200 units should be valued *a*
cost (£6 each) as this is lower than current cost (£8 each). 80
units costing £9 each were bought on 23rd November, none o
which has yet been sold. The price of these is *higher* than the pric
at 31st December, *i.e.* £9 as against £8. We should, therefor
value these goods at the lower figure of £8. The 600 units bough
on 31st December for £8 each will be valued at that price since cos
and current market value are the same.

Chapter IX

7

TRIAL BALANCE

	Debit	Credit
Goods for resale	388	
Typewriter	75	
Repairs	125	
Sales		58
Creditors—T. Jackson	91	
P. Sanders	148	
	—	23
Capital		45
Bank	441	
Debtors—V. Lewis	63	
K. Glover	75	
S. Gray	31	
C. Kingsley	54	
D. Phillips	17	
	—	
	240	
	£1,269	£1,26

8

Trial balance totals £2,039.
Gross profit, £239 Net profit, £97. Balance sheet totals, £1,517
Cost of sales, £300. Gross profit percentage = 44·34%.

a)

TRIAL BALANCE 14TH OCTOBER

Bank	£95	
Cash	7	
Purchases	450	
Sundries	12	
Wages	6	
Capital		£500
D. Hughes	340	
Sales		410
	£910	£910

Gross profit	£130
Net profit	£112
Balance sheet totals	£612

b)

TRIAL BALANCE AT 31ST OCTOBER

Capital (including net profit at 14th Oct.)		£612
Farmer		300
D. Hughes	140	
Purchases	300	
Sales		389
C. Heath	336	
Carriage	2	
Wages	6	
Bank	287	
Cash	12	
Rent	48	
Stock	170	
	£1,301	£1,301

Gross profit	£109
Net profit	£53
Balance sheet totals	£965

Chapter XI

Cash book, *debit* side: Total of "Discount allowed" (Memorandum)
column = £18·66.

Chapter X

ANALYSED PURCHASE DAY BOOK

	Bought ledger folio	Total	Purchase of goods	Light and heat	Rent, rates and insurance	Printing stationery and advertising	Telephone	Motor expns.	Repairs	Pvt. ledger
Apr 1 N. Rees		£10	£10							
3 Exton Elec. Board		32		£32						
4 Exton B. Council		84			£84					
5 B. Connor		27	27							
8 Baker Bros.		15				£15				
9 Charlton & Co. Ltd.		58		58						
10 L. Perkins Ltd.		109	109							
12 J. Millington		22	22							
13 Exton Gas Board		41		41						
16 Lincoln & Sons		89	89							
17 Clay & Co. Ltd.		28			28					
19 Sinclair Ltd.		34				34				
20 A. Landlord		120			120					
23 Fielding & Co.		65	65							
24 Exton Garage		23						£23		
25 Post Office		29					£29			
26 Office Supplies Co.		95								£95
28 Exton Press Ltd.		14				14				
29 L. Harrington		38							£38	
30 S. Neil		55	55							
30 Exton Garage Ltd.		17						17		
		£1,005	£377	£131	£232	£63	£29	£40	£38	£95

6

Private ledger: the Discount Allowed Account will be *debited* with the total of the Memorandum column, *i.e.* £18·66. The *corresponding credit* will be found in the various personal accounts of the customers concerned, *i.e.* the appropriate sum being credited in each case.

9

Cash book, *credit* side: Total of "Discounts received" (Memorandum) column = £12·51.

Private ledger: £12·51 will be *credited* to the Discount Received Account. The individual amounts making up this total will be *debited* to the accounts of the respective suppliers in the bought ledger.

Chapter XII

5

Trial balance totals = £11,439

6

Trial balance totals	= £27,945
Capital	= £1,059
Gross profit	= £7,853
Net profit	= £2,867
Balance sheet totals	= £3,713

7

(*a*) The trial balance totals are not affected. The Light and Heat Account should be £435 and "Drawings" figure £2,393.

(*b*) Reduce the debit side by £33, increase the credit side by £33.

(*c*) Add £50 to the credit side.

(*d*) Add £14 to the credit side.

(*e*) Add £31 to the debit side.

The corrected trial balance totals should read £29,976.

Chapter XIII

7

Capital expenditure may be defined as any expenditure on the purchase of assets which are to be employed in a business and which by their nature have the characteristics of permanence. They are not purchased, therefore, *for resale*.

Revenue expenditure, on the other hand, comprises all those expenses which are necessarily incurred in the day-to-day running of a business and the benefit of which is transient. They are mainly connected with the rendering of services of one kind or another, *e.g.* light and heat, telephone, salaries, advertising, insurance, etc.

8

The effect on the balance sheet of:

(*a*) would be to increase the assets side by an additional £200 of stock and to increase the liabilities by the addition of a like amount to the creditors;

(*b*) would be a decrease in the value of machinery owned by £350 and a like decrease in the Capital Account;

(*c*) would show an *increase* of the asset "Machinery" and a *decrease* of the asset "Cash at bank" by £600 in each case. There would be no alteration in the total of either the assets or the liabilities;

(*d*) would be to *decrease* the assets by £1,000 by the elimination of this deposit at the Savings Bank and equally on the liabilities side there would be a *decrease* in the balance of the Capital Account.

9

The items of capital expenditure are:

Quarterly H.P. instalment on gas-fired furnace (but see Note below)	£8·2
New gas fire	14·8

All the other items would be regarded as being revenue expenditure. The accounts to be opened would be for:

Lighting and heating	£14·4 + £18·7	(debit)
Hire of equipment	£2·0	(,,)
Repairs and maintenance	£3·0 + £3·5	(,,)
Gas Furnace	£8·2	(,,)
Fixtures and fittings	£14·8	(,,)
Northern Gas Board	£64·6	(credit)

NOTE: There would unquestionably be an element of interest included in the payment of the hire-purchase instalment on the gas-fired furnace. Suppose that the charge for interest amounted to £1·20. The correct treatment for this would be to credit £1·20 to the Gas Furnace Account and to debit a similar amount to Hire-Purchase Interest Account because this item is regarded as "revenue expenditure." The rest of the payment, *i.e.* £7, is "capital expenditure."

Chapter XIV

Motor Vehicle Account

19–2			19–2			
Jan. 1	Bank A/c	£2,400	Dec. 31	Depreciation A/c		£600
			31	Balance c/d		1,800
		£2,400				£2,400
19–3			19–3			
Jan. 1	Balance b/d	1,800	Dec. 31	Depreciation A/c		450
				Balance c/d		1,350
		£1,800				£1,800
19–4						
Jan. 1	Balance b/d	£1,350				

Machine Account

19–2		
Apr. 1	Bank A/c	£3,000

Provision for Depreciation Account

		19–2		
		Sept. 30	Depreciation A/c	£200
		19–3		
		Sept. 30	„	400
		19–4		
		Sept. 30	„	400
				£1,000

NOTE: The depreciation is calculated upon the cost (£3,000) *less* the estimated residual value (£200), *i.e.* a net figure of £2,800 over 7 years.

Chapter XV

6

Gross profit	= £4,761
Net profit	= £3,330
Balance sheet totals	= £33,346

7

Gross profit	= £1,290 (33·33%)
Net profit	= £784
Balance sheet totals	= £3,076

8

Net profit per the draft accounts =		£4,02?
Add: (a) Cost of cement mixer wrongly charged in in P. & L. A/c		15?
(d) Private rates wrongly charged in P. & L. A/c		14?
(e) Wages charged in P. & L. A/c for proprietor's *private* garage		12?
		£4,44?
Less: (b) Drawings wrongly debited with the charge for the road fund tax of van	£50	
(f) Goods not debited in the Purchases Account	89	13?
		£4,30?

The item in (c) does not affect the profit.

Chapter XVI

8

Profit and Loss Account

Provision for doubtful debts	£89	Net profit (as per question)	£2,87?
Net profit—*adjusted*	2,784		
	£2,873		£2,87?
		Balance b/d	2,78?

Provision for Doubtful Debts Account

Balance c/d	£89	Profit and Loss A/c (5% of £1,780)	£89
	£89		£89
		Balance b/d	£89

BALANCE SHEET (EXTRACT)

	Assets Sundry debtors £1,780 *Less* Provision for doubtful debts 89	
		£1,691

Provision for Doubtful Debts Account

19-4 Mar. 31	Balance c/d (5% of £16,000)	£800	19-3 Mar. 31	Profit and Loss A/c	£450
			19-4 Mar. 31	Profit and Loss A/c (increase in provision to make it up to 5% of £16,000)	350
		£800			£800
			19-4 Apr. 1	Balance b/d	£800

Bad Debts Account

19-4			19-4		
Mar. 31	Debtors Accounts (Bad debts written off during *this* year)	£420	Mar. 31	Debtors Accounts (Bad debts written off *in the previous year* now recovered)	£6(
			Mar. 31	Profit and Loss A/c (Net amount written off)	£36(
		£420			£42(

Profit and Loss Account 31st March, 19-4

Provision for doubtful debts	£350	
Bad debts written off	360	
	£710	

Alternative method

In some cases the business may employ an alternative metho(and use *one account only* for both the bad debts written off and fo: any provision deemed to be prudent. If we applied it to this cas(we would have the following position for the year ended 31s' March 19-4.

Bad Debts Account

19-4			19-3		
Mar. 31	Debtors Accounts (writings off)	£420	Apr. 1	Balance b/d	£45(
Mar. 31	Balance c/d (5% of £16,000)	800	19-4		
			Mar. 31	Debtors Accounts (recoveries)	6(
			Mar. 31	Profit and Loss A/c	71(
		£1,220			£1,22(
			19-4		
			Apr. 1	Balance b/d	£80(

Profit and Loss Account

Bad debts	£710	

It can be seen that whichever method is employed the total amount to be debited in the Profit and Loss Account is £710.

Chapter XVII

5

Provision for Discounts Received

Jan. 1	Balance b/d	£390	Dec. 31	Balance c/d	£540
Dec. 31	Profit and Loss A/c	150			
		£540			£540
	Balance b/d	£540			

Profit and Loss Account

	Provision for discount received	£150

Trading and Profit and Loss Account

		£2,000			£24,310
Stock			Sales		
Purchases	20,220		*Less:* Returns		290
Less: Returns	140				
		20,080			24,020
Carriage inwards		720	Stock		3,100
		22,800			
Gross profit		4,320			
		£27,120			£27,120
Salaries	730	762	Gross profit		4,320
	+32		Rent received		160
	580				
Rates and insurance	−160				
		420			
Advertising		103			
Carriage on sales		200			
Bad debts w/off		74			
Increase in provision for doubtful debts		25			
Depreciation:					
Office equipment	81				
Shop fittings	600				
		681			
Provision for discount allowed		34			
		2,299			
Net profit		2,181			
		£4,480			£4,480

BALANCE SHEET

					£4,000
Capital:			Premises		
Balance at start	£10,170		Office equipment	£810	
Add: Net profit	2,181		*Less:* Depreciation	281	
	£12,351				529
Less: Drawings	1,480		Shop fittings	4,800	
		£10,871	*Less:* Depreciation	1,400	
Trade creditors	1,070				3,400
Accrued expenses	32		Stock		3,100
Bank overdraft	870		Debtors	£1,700	
		1,972	*Less:*		
			Provisions		
			£85 + 34 119		
				1,581	
			Prepayments	160	
			Cash	73	
					4,914
		£12,843			£12,843

Chapter XVIII

0

Chalmers and Son

	19–1		19–2	
Fixed Assets				
Plant at cost	£40,000		£60,000	
Less: Depreciation	18,300		24,500	
		£21,700		£35,500
Transport at cost	5,000		6,000	
Less: Depreciation	2,400		3,900	
		2,600		2,100
		24,300		37,600
Current Assets				
Stock	7,138		10,243	
Debtors	5,209		7,116	
Bank	4,163		4,294	
	16,510		21,653	
Less: Current liabilities	9,478		11,134	
Working Capital		7,032		10,519
Capital Employed		£31,332		£48,119

Represented by the following sources of finance:

Capital	£31,332	43,119
Bank Loan	—	5,000
	£31,332	£48,119

1

(a)	Capital employed	£41,000
(b)	Current assets	23,500
(c)	Current liabilities	8,000
(d)	Working capital	15,500

12

Murlow

	19–4	19–5
	£	£
(a) Current assets	42,000	45,000
Current liabilities	21,000	30,000
Working capital	21,000	15,000
Working capital ratio	2 : 1	3 : 2

(b) The opening working capital ratio is quite high; it is still satisfactory at end of 19–5, but it is much less well balanced with the substantial decline in the bank balance. The reduction in the working capital ratio is caused by the heavy long-term investment only partly covered by long-term finance; the reduction in liquidity has been reinforced by the heavy investment in stock.

13

(a) Funds flow statement

	31st December 19–8	31st December 19–9	Source	Use
Assets	£	£	£	£
Buildings	6,000	6,000		
Plant (after depreciation)	3,000	4,200		1,200
Motor Vans (after depreciation)	1,750	1,400	350	
Stocks	3,250	4,175		925
Debtors	2,840	2,620	220	
Cash at bank	2,780	910	1,870	
	£19,620	£19,305		
Financed by				
Owner's capital (Balance at 1st January 19–8)	5,420	5,420		
Add: Profit for year		8,690	8,690	
		14,110		
Less: Drawings		4,355		4,355
		9,755		
Loan from bank	10,000	4,500		5,500
Creditors	4,200	5,050	850	
	£19,620	£19,305	£11,980	£11,980

(b) Individual changes in working capital

	Source £	Use £
Stocks		925
Debtors	220	
Bank	1,870	
Creditors	850	
Net application of funds		2,015
	£2,940	£2,940

(c) Working Capital	19–8	19–9
Current assets	8,870	7,705
Current liabilities	4,200	5,050
	£4,670	£2,655

Reduction in working capital £2,015

(d) Reconciliation

Working Capital at start (31st December 19–8)		4,670
Add: Profit	8,690	
Depreciation on Motor Vans	350	
		9,040
		13,710
Less: Cost of new plant (net)	1,200	
Drawings	4,355	
Bank loan repaid	5,500	
		11,055
Working Capital at end (31st December 19–9)		£2,655

APPENDIX III

BIBLIOGRAPHY

Stott, J. Randall: *An Introduction to Accounts*, Edward Arnold (Publishers) Ltd.

Harold C. Edey: *Introduction to Accounting*, Hutchinson University Library.

Favell, A. J.: *Practical Book Keeping and Accounts*, University Tutorial Press Ltd.

Castle, E. F. and Owens, N. P.: *Principles of Accounts*, Macdonald and Evans Ltd.

Baston, Andrew: *Elements of Accounts*, Cassell and Co. Ltd.

Magee, C. C.: *Framework of Accountancy*, Macdonald and Evans Ltd.

Castle, E. F.: *Principles of Accounts*, University Tutorial Press

INDEX

M&E Handbooks

Law

'A' Level Law/B Jones
Basic Law/L B Curzon
Cases in Banking Law/P A Gheerbrant, D Palfreman
Cases in Company Law/M C Oliver
Cases in Contract Law/W T Major
Commercial and Industrial Law/A R Ruff
Company Law/M C Oliver, E Marshall
Constitutional and Administrative Law/I N Stevens
Consumer Law/M J Leder
Conveyancing Law/P H Kenny, C Bevan
Criminal Law/L B Curzon
Equity and Trusts/L B Curzon
Family Law/P J Pace
General Principles of English Law/P W D Redmond, J Price, I N Stevens
Jurisprudence/L B Curzon
Labour Law/M Wright, C J Carr
Land Law/L B Curzon
Landlord and Tenant/J M Male
Law of Banking/D Palfreman
Law of Evidence/L B Curzon
Law of Torts/J G M Tyas
Meetings: Their Law and Practice/L Hall, P Lawton, E Rigby
Mercantile Law/P W D Redmond, R G Lawson
Private International Law/A W Scott
Sale of Goods/W T Major
The Law of Contract/W T Major

Business and Management

Advanced Economics/G L Thirkettle
Advertising/F Jefkins
Applied Economics/E Seddon, J D S Appleton
Basic Economics/G L Thirkettle
Business Administration/L Hall
Business and Financial Management/B K R Watts
Business Organisation/R R Pitfield
Business Mathematics/L W T Stafford
Business Systems/R G Anderson
Business Typewriting/S F Parks
Computer Science/J K Atkin
Data Processing Vol 1: Principles and Practice/R G Anderson
Data Processing Vol 2: Information Systems and Technology/R G Anderson
Economics for 'O' Level/L B Curzon
Elements of Commerce/C O'Connor
Human Resources Management/H T Graham
Industrial Administration/J C Denyer, J Batty
International Marketing/L S Walsh
Management, Planning and Control/R G Anderson
Management – Theory and Principles/T Proctor
Managerial Economics/J R Davies, S Hughes
Marketing/G B Giles
Marketing Overseas/A West
Marketing Research/T Proctor, M A Stone
Microcomputing/R G Anderson
Modern Commercial Knowledge/L W T Stafford
Modern Marketing/F Jefkins
Office Administration/J C Denyer, A L Mugridge
Operational Research/W M Harper, H C Lim
Organisation and Methods/R G Anderson
Production Management/H A Harding
Public Administration/M Barber, R Stacey
Public Relations/F Jefkins
Purchasing/C K Lysons
Sales and Sales Management/P Allen
Statistics/W M Harper
Stores Management/R J Carter

Accounting and Finance

Auditing/L R Howard
Basic Accounting/J O Magee
Basic Book-keeping/J O Magee
Capital Gains Tax/V Di Palma
Company Accounts/J O Magee
Company Secretarial Practice/L Hall, G M Thom
Cost and Management Accounting – Vols 1 & 2/W M Harper
Elements of Banking/D P Whiting
Elements of Finance for Managers/B K R Watts
Elements of Insurance/D S Hansell
Finance of Foreign Trade/D P Whiting
Investment: A Practical Approach/D Kerridge
Practice of Banking/E P Doyle, J E Kelly
Principles of Accounts/E F Castle, N P Owens
Taxation/H Toch

Humanities and Science

Biology Advanced Level/P T Marshall
British Government and Politics/F Randall
Chemistry for 'O' Level/G Usher
Economic Geography/H Robinson
European History 1789–1914/C A Leeds
Introduction to Ecology/J C Emberlin
Land Surveying/R J P Wilson
Modern Economic History/E Seddon
Political Studies/C A Leeds
Sociology 'O' Level/F Randall
Twentieth Century History 1900–45/C A Leeds
World History: 1900 to the Present Day/C A Leeds

KJ6